How to Make Soap

A Complete Step-by-Step Soap-Making Guide for Beginners

By: Rebecca Wellner

Text Copyright © Lightbulb Publishing

All rights reserved. No part of this guide may be reproduced in any form without permission in writing from the publisher except in the case of brief quotations embodied in critical articles or reviews.

Legal & Disclaimer

The information in this book and its contents are not designed to replace or substitute any form of medical or professional advice. It is not intended to replace the need for independent medical, financial, legal, or other professional advice or services as may be required. The content and information in this book have been provided for educational and entertainment purposes only.

The content and information in this book have been compiled from reliable sources and are accurate to the best of the Author's knowledge, information, and belief. However, the Author cannot guarantee the accuracy and validity and cannot be held liable for errors and/or omissions. Furthermore, changes are made periodically to this book as and when needed.

Where appropriate and/or necessary, you must consult a professional (including but not limited to your doctor, attorney, financial advisor, or such other professional advisor) before using any of the suggested remedies, techniques, or information in this book.

Upon using the contents and information in this book, you agree to hold harmless the Author from and against any damages, costs, and expenses, including any legal fees potentially resulting from the application of any of the information provided. This disclaimer applies to any loss, damages, or injury caused by the use and application, whether directly or indirectly, of any advice or information presented, whether for breach of contract, tort, negligence, personal injury, criminal intent, or under any other cause of action.

You agree to accept all the risks of using the information presented in this book.

You agree by continuing to read this book that, where appropriate and/or necessary, you shall consult a professional (including but not limited to your doctor, attorney, financial advisor, or such other advisor as needed) before using any of the suggested remedies, techniques, or information in this book.

Table of Contents

Introduction

I want to congratulate you on purchasing this book. Perhaps you're interested in learning something new or just want your own beautiful bar of soap sans chemicals. Whatever the reason, I assure you that it's your first step towards changing your perception of cosmetic products.

Soap-making is an art that can only be practiced with hard work and patience. Like any art form, you must hone your skills until you master it. But even your first bar of soap can give you immense happiness. Not only have you learned something new, but you're also keeping your family safe from all the horrid chemicals that are used in soaps these days.

This book contains a detailed explanation to help you experiment and make your own recipes. Although soap-making is pretty easy once you get the hang of it, it's essential to be safe. And that's exactly why you need to understand the ingredients that go into your soap.

Needless to say, this book might even inspire you to take up soap making as a commercial venture. Handmade soaps are all the rage these days, and there's nothing more fulfilling than pampering your family and friends with natural goodness that is both beautiful and safe.

I hope you enjoy the book and get to the point where you make your own recipes rather than simply copying the ones found online.

Chapter 1
Basics of Soap Making

Soap-making is not for the faint of heart. Somewhere along the line, you might ask the question, "Why make soap at all?" It's easy to buy soaps in bulk and still keep your budget in line at your nearest big box store. However, you could be compromising your health in the process.

Have you ever wondered why the bars you buy at chain stores aren't even labeled as soap? Have you ever noticed? They are usually called beauty bars or moisturizing bars. For the FDA to recognize it as soap, it must be a byproduct of a chemical reaction between oils and fats with an alkali. The product must be able to clean effectively solely due to the byproduct, but since the soaps made commercially are actually detergents disguised as soaps, they cannot be classified as soaps.

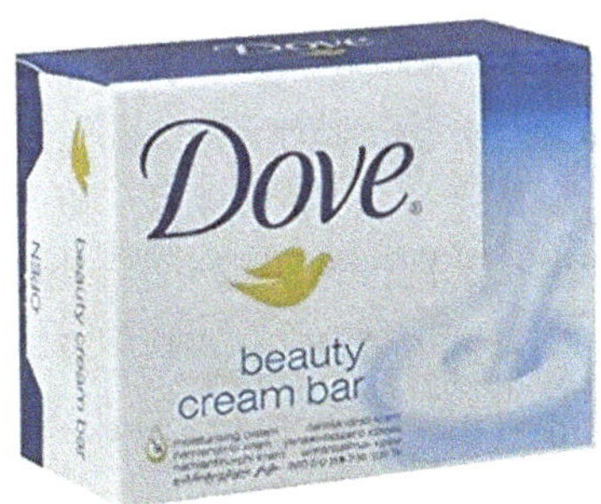

Because commercial soaps are actually detergents, they will strip your body of its natural oils. In fact, commercially made soaps work similarly to the detergent used on your clothes, which is great at removing oils. In fact, those soaps don't even contain glycerin, the component in soaps that actually moisturizes your body. All of the glycerin is removed from these "soaps," leaving your skin super dry, itchy, and vulnerable.

Additionally, chemicals are added to bars that are re-batched again and again to make it as good as new. And that's not even to mention the types of fragrances they use, fragrances that are carcinogenic and can cause serious problems over time.

Soap making isn't difficult, and you don't need to use too many chemicals to produce good quality soaps. Plus, you have the peace of mind that you're using something handmade, natural, and safe for you and the rest of your family.

What if I told you that you could make natural soaps and not burn a hole in your wallet? The process is quite simple, really. But it becomes truly easy when you understand the basics of making soap from scratch. Anyone can copy a recipe and make a basic product, but it will only get him or her so far. Mastering the craft of soap making, starting with the basics, will open a whole wide world of possibilities, not to mention the various business opportunities.

All your doubts will disappear once you hold handmade soap in your hands. The difference from a commercial soap, stripped of the goodness of products like glycerin, is immediately noticeable.

In a nutshell, soap is the result of a chemical reaction between lye and oils. Now, lye is dangerous, but that's exactly why you're going to take precautionary measures. If you are not comfortable using lye, there are melt-and-pour soaps that can be made without it. And, since there are so many ways of making soap, you can just let your creativity flow without any inhibitions. As long as you understand the basics of chemistry, making soap is easy.

Chemistry of Soap Making

You don't need to delve into the depths of chemistry to understand soap making; you'll do just fine if you understand the basics. To make soap, you only need to have a general idea of saponification – a term that's frequently used by soap makers, also called soapers.

What is Saponification?

To put it simply, saponification is the chemical reaction that occurs when a base and an acid react with each other to form salts. Soap, in its simplest form, is nothing but a salt. So, for instance, when you're mixing a fat or acid (olive oil, coconut oil, etc.) with an alkaline base like lye, you get salt or soap.

As long as the base contains one hydroxide ion, it will give you the desired reaction. Thus, you can use both sodium hydroxide (lye) and potassium hydroxide to make soap. While sodium hydroxide is generally used to produce hard soap, potassium hydroxide is used to make liquid soap. This book will not cover liquid soap, but the process becomes easy to understand if you have mastered the process of making hard soap.

On the subject of the fats or acids you will use, you must know that there are endless possible combinations used to make soap. You can choose anything from olive oil, castor oil, emu oil, or whatever other oils your heart desires. However, each and every fat you choose will react with the base or lye in a different manner. This is why you simply cannot substitute olive oil for coconut oil (or any other oil) and hope that you'll end up with a usable soap.

This also means that if you're following a particular recipe, you need to stick to the exact measurements and ingredients to achieve the final product. Of course, experienced soap makers don't worry when they use a few extra milliliters of water or oil because they have the experience needed to compensate for it. However, no matter how experienced a soap maker is, they do not start a recipe before calculating their measurements.

"Wow, this is too complicated," I hear you say. Now, you have to calculate the measurements. Well, yes, you need to do some basic calculations. However, it's actually extremely simple. There are even calculators for this exact purpose! I recommend using SoapCalc for your calculations. I'll explain the calculation in more detail in subsequent chapters.

Books on soap making and online classes teach you how to follow a recipe, but they don't tell you how to create your own recipes. And that's a shame. But since I believe in teaching you how to create your own soap rather than handing you a bunch of recipes, I'll make sure that you'll be able to design your own recipes by the time you're done with this book.

Chapter 2

Most Common Soap Making Processes

Many beginning soap makers will be apprehensive of lye, and with good reason. Thus, there are various ways of making soap if you really don't want anything to do with lye. Each process will be explained in greater detail in subsequent chapters, but here are five soap-making processes.

1) Melt and Pour

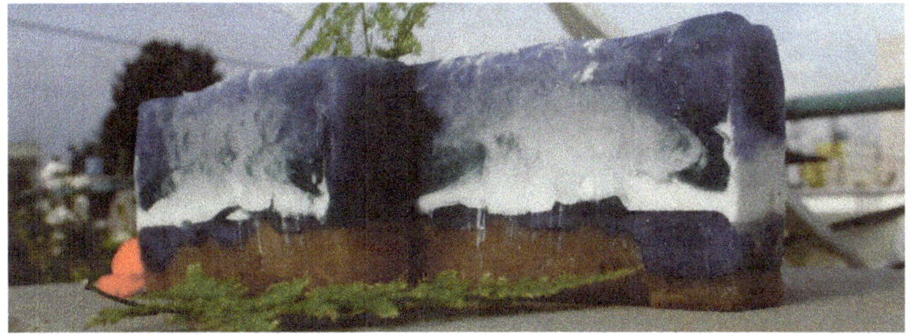

Melt and Pour soaps are the easiest of all. These soaps are a no-brainer if you're a beginner. The process is as simple as following the instructions on the label. You can think of it like a cake mix where you just combine the ingredients and prepare a wonderfully fragrant cake without fretting over the precise measurements of a recipe from scratch. All you need to do is cut the blocks into chunks, microwave them, mix in some color, and you have soap! Easy peasy!

2) Cold Process

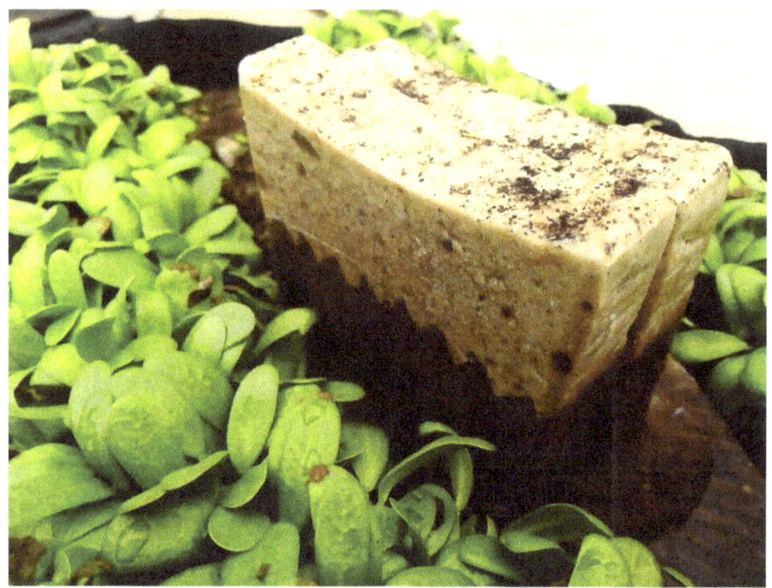

Cold Process soaps are a little harder than Melt and Pour. In this process, you make everything from scratch, including the batter. But it's not as difficult as you think. In fact, CP is considered by many to be the best way to make natural soaps. Want to make soap with mango? Including mango puree! How about papaya? Yeah, you could do that too! You can get as creative as you want with CP soaps.

Since people fear handling lye, they will avoid CP soaps, but it's actually easy if you follow all the safety precautions. The finished soap doesn't contain lye, so don't let fear hold you back. How many store-bought cake mixes will you bake before you start to wonder if you could make a better cake yourself? Not too many. Similarly, once you start off with Melt and Pour soaps, it's only a matter of time before you try Cold Process soaps.

3) Hot Process

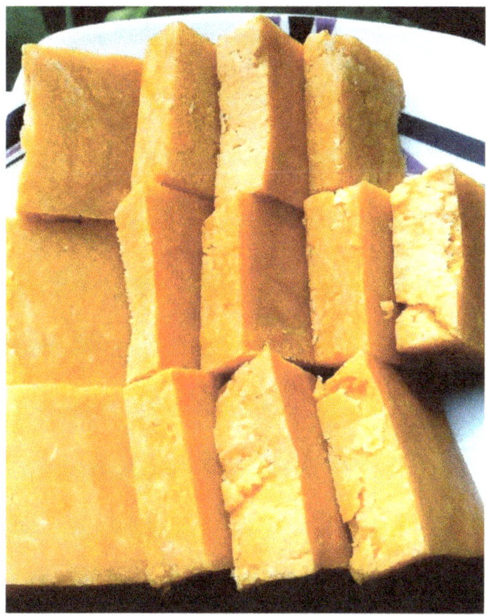

Hot Process is just like the Cold Process; however, rather than letting the soap cure (you'll understand all this later, I promise!), you're going to "cook" the soap yourself in a crockpot or pan first.

4) Cold Process Oven Process

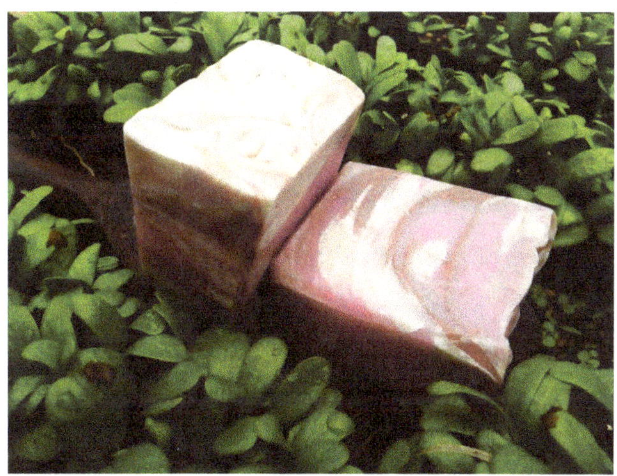

As the name suggests, it's a combination of Cold Process and Oven Process. You start off like it's Cold Process, but you cook it immediately rather than waiting for it to cure by itself.

5) Re-batching Soap

This is a process where you turn your old, unused soap bars into shiny, new, beautiful ones. You simply shred the old soaps but add extra character through fragrance, colors, etc.

Which process is the easiest?

With so many different methods of making soap, most people will obviously want to start with the easiest. Although M&P (Melt and Pour) is easiest overall, many people start with Cold Process. However, if you have children or pets and don't want to deal with lye, M&P is the best choice.

For M&P, you buy pre-made blocks of soap and cut them into smaller pieces. Then, you melt the chunks in the microwave or a double boiler. Always remember not to use direct heat because you'll end up with charred, not melted, soap.

Once everything is melted down, you apply the fragrance and colors of your choice and pour the melted soap into molds. Unlike CP (Cold Process) soap, M&P can be used immediately!

So, let's understand the pros and cons of each method.

Melt and Pour Soap

Advantages

- Perfect for beginners.

- Super easy and quick to make.

- Doesn't take a lot of effort, and even children can experiment with it under supervision.

- In as little as three hours, you can have soap bars fully hardened and ready for use.

- There's no issue of ricing or seizing, unlike CP soap, and you're free to use your choice of fragrance oils.

- M&P soaps hold fragrance better in comparison with CP soaps since the saponification process is already complete.

- Perfect for those yearning to decorate their soaps with glitter, as the colors really pop!

- Cleaning up is super easy as there's no lye. And since the container is just soap, you only need to rinse it off, and you're done!

Disadvantages

- Due to the extra glycerin, M&P soaps tend to "sweat" and become slippery.

- You cannot customize the base or add extra oils.

- You also cannot add fresh ingredients or deviate too much from your manufacturer's instructions.

- The base melts and hardens very quickly, and you won't have a lot of time to get as creative as you can with CP soaps.

- Not as luxurious or creamy as CP soaps.

- It's pretty easy to burn the base if you heat it more than required.

Cold Process soap

Advantages

- You are in complete control of everything from the very beginning.

- Produces hard bars of soap that last a long time.

- You can make any soap according to your preference.

- Gives you the freedom to add fresh ingredients such as fruit juice, milk, etc.

- No harmful chemicals.

- Produces a very creamy and rich luxurious lather.

- Allows you to create any design you want.

Disadvantages

- Takes a long time (24-48 hours) for the soap to harden once poured into molds.

- Takes an even longer time to cure (4 to 6 weeks) once the soap is released from the mold.

- Cannot be used without curing or until the saponification process is complete.

- Not all fragrance oils react well to CP soap and can cause ricing and seizing of the soap.

- Takes more time in comparison with M&P soap and HP soap.

- Requires you to be very careful since you're dealing with lye.

- CP soaps don't hold the fragrance as well because it fades away as the soap completes its saponification process.

- Cleaning up can be messy, especially due to the use of lye.

- Lye will burn your skin, so it's not possible to make CP without taking safety measures.

Hot Process Soap

Advantages

- Hot Process is very much like CP. The difference is that you manually cook the soap before pouring it into the mold.

- It can be used right away as soon as you cut the soap – just like M&P.

- It allows you to customize oils according to your preference. For example, olive oil can be used for moisturizing, and coconut oil for lather. However, although you can add fresh ingredients such as milk and sugar, these ingredients tend to burn as the soap is cooked.

- Produces beautiful bars of soap that look and feel rustic. Although some may prefer the smooth texture of CP soaps, HP soaps are alluring in their own way.

- Easy and quick to make.

- As natural as it gets since you have control over every ingredient added.

- Cleaning up after you make the soap is easy, as there's no lye left behind.

Disadvantages

- Hot Process is just an extension of CP soap, so you'll still need to deal with lye while making the batter at the beginning.

- Doesn't allow you to create swirls or other intricate designs due to its thick texture.

- Fragrance oils should be added at the very last minute, or you risk burning them.

- Requires you to keep an eye on the soap as it cooks and expands.

- Overheating the soap batter can result in soap overflowing from the mold, commonly known as a soap volcano.

- Soap batter can overflow if you add anything containing sugar, including ingredients such as milk or honey.

Chapter 3

Tools and Ingredients

You don't need sophisticated tools and ingredients to make soaps. In fact, simple and fewer ingredients can give you great results. For example, one of the simplest recipes has soapers combine olive oil with lye and water to make castile soap, which is an excellent soap for babies.

Baby soaps are usually expensive, but you can make tons of castile soap for just a few bucks. And nothing beats castile soaps because there are no extra additives or chemicals that can irritate your baby's skin. You can use them too! I bet you'll love them!

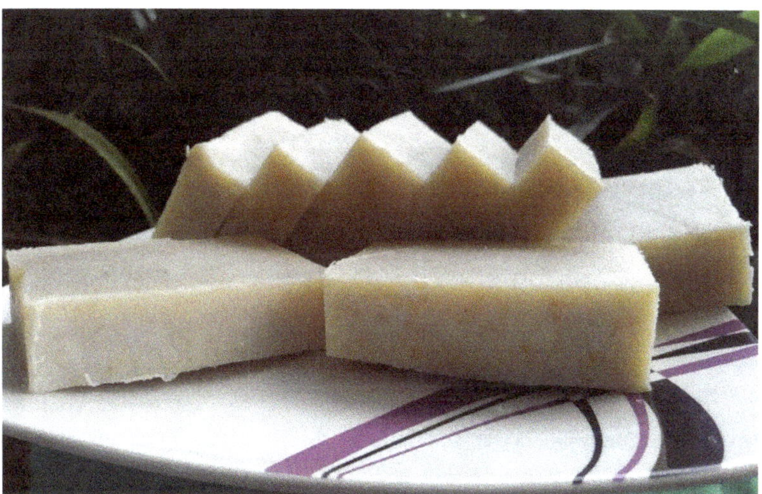

These are freshly cut castile soaps made with olive oil and oats! They will look gorgeous after they are cured and beveled.

Soap-making requires a few specific tools that are commonly found in the kitchen. Some people will reuse the same tools to prepare food after making soap. Generally speaking, it is safer to only use your tools for soap making, even though, in most cases, no harm will come to you as you are only making soap with them. Still, I advise you to keep your soap and your food as separate as possible.

Take a look at the tools that are important:

1) **Safety Equipment** – Gloves and goggles are your friends when it comes to making soap. If you want to try making HP or CP soap, you absolutely must wear them. If you think that you can wing it and make soap without the proper protection, you are wrong! Lye can easily splatter up from your blender and get into your eyes. And, boy, does it sting! If you are safe, then soap making can be very fun, but lye can and will burn your skin. You should wear full-sleeved shirts, goggles, and gloves. You'll be safe and all set to make some amazing soaps.

2) **Containers to make soap** – Many people love crockpots for making soaps because it's a hassle-free process. A crockpot big enough to hold at least 10 to 12 quarts will yield loads of soap. However, crockpots are only useful if you're going to cook the soap, like in the Hot Process. If you don't already have a crockpot, you can also use a steel container or pot. Many people, myself included, make do with steel containers, and these work amazingly well, too. One more option is glass containers if you have any Pyrex bowls lying around.

Never use aluminum containers or utensils to make any kind of soap, as the lye tends to eat through the containers and make them useless.

Make sure that you use steel utensils when making soap. Plastic utensils will also work fine, but use them with caution. The lye can corrode the plastic if it's not high quality. As long as you watch the soap while it's cooking, you'll be fine.

3) **Blender** – Making soap takes time. As such, the saponification process can wear you out if you plan to mix the lye and oils manually. I recommend using a blender that thoroughly combines the mixture to ensure that there's no free lye remaining. You can stir your soap batter with a spatula if a blender isn't in your budget, but you'll spend at least 20-25 minutes extra doing a job that would take the blender 3 minutes. I assure you it will be worth the investment.

4) **Scales** – Now, this is truly a must. You cannot eyeball the ingredients, or you'll end up with a mess and no soap to clean it! A digital scale that measures both grams and ounces will be perfect, as you should never measure ingredients by volume when making soap. Most recipes for soaps will require measurements in grams, so it's important that your scale can weigh both. Remember that you need to weigh not only the oils in large quantities but fragrance oils in small quantities, too. Therefore, a scale with the capacity to measure anything from 0.03 ounces to at least 176 ounces will work well. That's from 1 gram to 5 liters or kilos.

An important note when you are using scales: make sure to always "tare" your scales. This means that you will place your measuring container on the scale and reset it to zero before measuring your ingredients. This way, you aren't including the weight of the container in your measurements.

5) **Bowls** – You'll need several bowls to hold water, oils, and fragrance oils. Both glass and plastic bowls can be used without a change in the quality of the finished product, but it's more economical to use plastic. Some people like to mix colors in separate bowls depending on the design they are creating, so it's good to have extra bowls on hand.

6) **Thermometer** – Temperature plays an essential role in making soap, so this one's a must-have. The oils and lye need to be mixed at specific temperatures. I personally love using a digital laser thermometer because you don't have to dip it into the oils and lye. And they are cheap to boot! But any steel thermometer will do fine.

7) **Spatulas** – Of course, you could use whisks and spoons to mix and scrap out your bowls, but silicone spatulas are amazing for soap-making because they get all the bits of oil and lye out of your container. They are perfect for mixing as well.

8) **Soap molds** – Obviously, you need molds to pour the soap into. There are so many types and so many designs that you'll have a tough time choosing one. I would recommend starting with the usual rectangular wooden molds with silicone liners. However, these molds can be a bit expensive. If you want to

save some money while you are starting out, try looking for videos that demonstrate how molds can be made out of unexpected materials, even cardboard! You could even use PVC pipes to make round soaps if you wanted! If you're extra hands-on, you can take the time to make your own wooden mold and never look back!

Ingredients

Now, we head on to the fun part – selecting your ingredients. After all, they can make or break your soap. The ingredients you choose depend on the type of soap you need. For instance, while you may prefer a soap with extra moisturizing abilities, someone else may love something with extra cleansing properties. The oils you choose will add character to your soap, and that's why you see soapers adding different types of oils.

Olive oil is a common ingredient used in soap making, but it doesn't produce a lot of lather. On the other hand, a soap made with lots of coconut oil cleans dirt really well and also produces big bubbles, but it doesn't make your skin softer like olive oil does. Avocado oil is amazing, but it's expensive. As you can see, the ingredients that you choose will have a major effect on the final product.

So, try to understand how to formulate a soap by familiarizing yourself with the following ingredients.

Ingredients

1) **Lye** – Lye, or sodium hydroxide, has already been mentioned several times in this book. You can't make soap without lye unless you're using pre-made bases, so lye is an essential ingredient. Lye is a harmful chemical and should be treated with caution, but as long as you stick to proper measurements, your finished soaps will not contain lye. You're probably imagining slathering yourself with soap that is full of lye, but, no, it's easy to discern whether a bar of soap is good or not.

   The only difference between solid and liquid soaps is that sodium hydroxide, lye, is used for solid soaps, while potassium hydroxide is best for liquid soaps.

2) **Water** – The second most important ingredient to make soap is water. While many people are okay with using tap water for their soaps, I recommend that you use distilled water. Why? Tap water contains salts that may interfere with your soap-making, whereas distilled water is stripped of minerals and gives you exactly the soap you want every time.

   It's also important to measure the amount of water properly. If you add too much water, it will take ages for the soap to cure, and if you don't add enough water, you may leave lye residues in the soap.

3) **Oils** – As mentioned earlier, the type of oils you choose will determine the characteristics and quality of your soap. But this doesn't mean that expensive oils equate to high-quality soap. For instance, sweet almond oil can be used to make a

great bar of soap, but olive oil will do the job just as well. Also, sweet almond oil is expensive, and you'll soon be spending a lot more than you intended if you use only premium oils. Oils such as avocado, sweet almond, papaya, watermelon seed, etc. are considered premium oils.

Palm oil, coconut oil, castor oil, olive oil, etc., are the most commonly used oils. However, there is a limit to the percentage of each type of oil that can be used in any given recipe. For instance, while a 100% olive oil soap will turn out amazing, a 100% castor oil soap will be nothing but a slippery mess.

Many soapers will use lard as a substitute for coconut oil, and you won't believe the beautiful soaps it produces! Even different kinds of butter, such as mango, cocoa, kokum, and shea butter, will produce hard bars of soap with lots of moisturizing properties.

Also, the ingredients you choose depend on whom you are making the soap. Is it for a friend or a customer? Your customers may prefer creamy soaps with lots of lather, but you probably love rock-hard soaps that last a long, long time and have amazing cleansing properties. The type of water used (hard or soft water) will also play a role in how the soap actually performs.

As you can understand, a lot of factors should be considered when choosing oils. So, how do you create the perfect recipe that appeals to almost everyone? Is it even possible? Yes, it is.

If you understand the fatty acid profile of the oils, everything becomes easier.

Here are a few guidelines to keep in mind while formulating recipes:

a) To increase a soap's moisturizing abilities

- Try using a lot of olive oil

- Replace water with other liquids like milk (goat, cow, and even breast milk!) and other dairy products like yogurt

- Replace water with fresh aloe juice for CP and HP soaps

- Increase the super fat (a term I'll explain later) to increase the conditioning properties

- Add at least 5-10% of moisturizing oils like avocado, olive, sweet almond, jojoba, rice bran, pumpkin seed oil, etc.

b) To increase the lather or bubbles

- Decrease the super fat as too much oil reduces lather

- Use oils that produce loads of lather, like coconut, babassu, palm oil, etc.

- Replace water with sugar-containing ingredients like milk, beer or wine

- Use sodium lactate to produce a hard bar of soap and increase bubbles

- Avoid using oils like olive oil that reduce lather

c) To make a rock-hard soap

- Reduce soft oils that make the soap softer and instead use oils like coconut with a combination of soft oils (Note – using 100% coconut oil will produce laundry soap, and that's extremely drying on your skin, so make sure you get the ratio right. 65% Coconut oil with a combination of other soft oils (olive+rice bran+castor oil will do the trick)

- Use stearic acid at the rate of 1% of the total formula

- Add hard butter, such as cocoa

- Add hard wax, such as beeswax, at the rate of 1-5% of the total formula

- Add sodium lactate (one teaspoon per pound of soap)

Remember that the final soap will depend on the percentage of hard and soft oils you've used. But oils are oils, right? What's the difference between hard and soft oils?

Hard oils

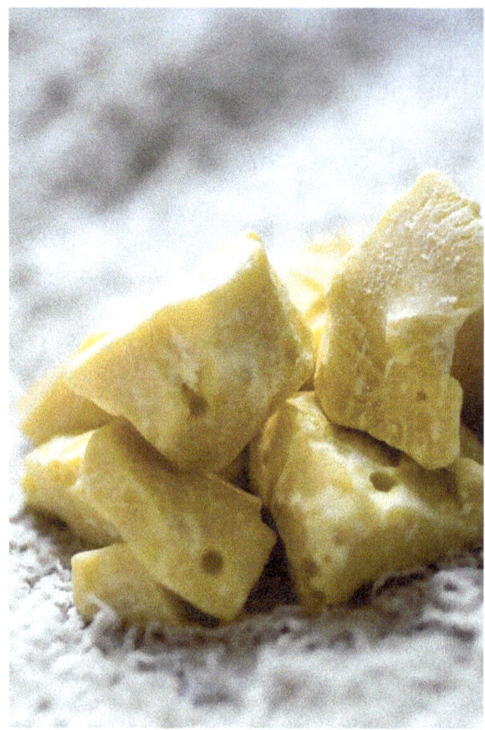

Cocoa Butter

Oils that are generally solid at normal room temperatures are considered hard oils. Such oils can even be semi-solid, like coconut oil. Hard oils like coconut, palm, and babassu are great for increasing lather, whereas hard kinds of butter like cocoa, kokum, mango, and shea are perfect for moisturizing.

Soft oils

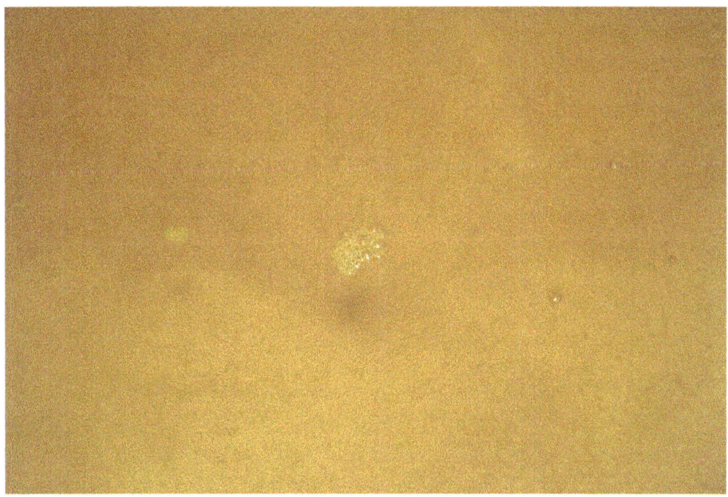

Conversely, soft oils are oils that are in a liquid form at room temperature. Remember that soft oils can make the soap too squishy. Thus, the right mix of both hard and soft oils is something you need to carefully consider. Oils like olive, castor, sunflower, rice bran, apricot kernel, and avocado are soft oils, though there are many other soft oils that can be included.

A special note on castor oil: Although high amounts of castor oil can make the soap too soft, there are no other oils matching its fatty acid profile, which is why it should be included in small percentages to ensure that the soap lathers beautifully.

4) **Fragrance** – What's a bar of soap without a bit of a lovely fragrance, eh? Of course, many people love soaps with no fragrance at all, whether it be due to preference or sensitivities. But many people enjoy using soaps that smell amazing.

The fragrances you select can not only do wonders for your body, but they can make you feel emotionally recharged as well. Selecting a good fragrance to make soap can't be done blindly because it depends on a few parameters, but it's not all that hard, either. Fragrances are generally available in two types – essential oils and fragrance oils. Depending on your budget and preference, you can choose either of the two and make great soap.

Essential oils – Essential oils are natural oils derived from either plants or flowers. They are aromatic, sensual, and extremely potent. You should never use essential oils directly on your skin. They are incredibly potent and will cause irritation. Unless it's already mixed with a carrier oil, you should never use essential oil directly on your skin.

Essential oils are available everywhere. Check with your local markets or online. However, be cautious about dupes. Check for reviews before you consider buying them. Now, since it's a tedious process to extract oils from plants, they are naturally expensive. The best part of working with essential oils is that they work perfectly with all kinds of soap-making processes.

Here's a list of some essential oils that can be used as a standalone product or combined with each other to derive amazing results.

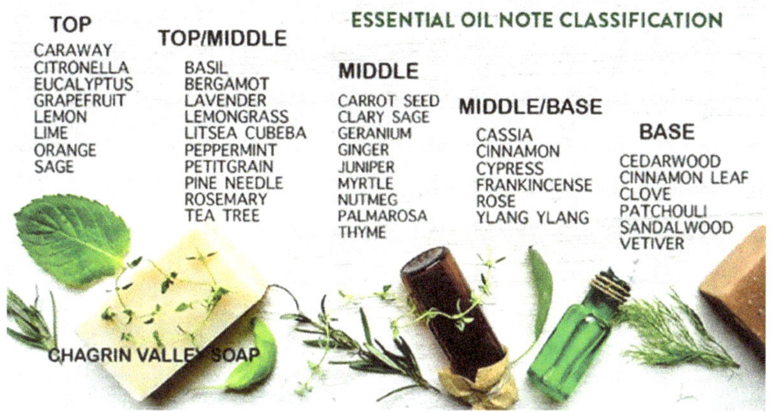

There's a caveat to using essential oils – they may not be ideal if you're producing large batches of soap. Unless your clients are specifically looking for essential oil soaps, they can burn a hole in your pocket if you use them in large quantities. For small batches, though, essential oils are perfect; it's like experiencing aromatherapy every day in the shower! Jasmine, patchouli, mint, lemon, orange, lavender, and rose are some of the most common essential oils that soapers use.

Fragrance oils – Unlike essential oils, fragrance oils are synthetic. Some of them are made with natural oils mixed with a synthetic fragrance. But they aren't really all that harmful. For instance, most of the perfumes you use are made of some kind of fragrance oil. So, if you're okay with using perfumes, you'll be okay with the fragrance oils as well. They are easily available and cost much less than essential oils.

One disadvantage of using fragrance oils is that they can cause the soap to misbehave. A common issue is the soap seizing up due to a component in the fragrance oil. They can also cause overheating, cause the soap to overflow from the mold, and harden the batter. These types of fragrances can wreak a lot of havoc. No matter how lovely some fragrances smell, there are certain fragrances that are best not used in soap. Floral fragrances are the usual suspects. For instance, gardenia fragrance oil has a heavenly smell, but using it in a batch of soap can be messy.

There are ways to salvage a batch of ruined soap, and you can even use fragrance oils that cause soap to misbehave to your advantage.

5) **Colors** – Choosing great colors can make your soap really stand out. Just imagine a dull soap sitting next to a vibrant soap with swirls in different colors! Which would you choose? People are naturally attracted to soaps that show off their colors. Liquid or solid – you get colors in several types. And don't forget to top off your soaps with glitter that blows your mind away! Unlike fragrances, colors won't affect the quality of the soap, so you're free to do whatever you want.

Like fragrances, colorants can also be distinguished into natural and lab-made colors.

Natural colors – When it comes to natural colorants, there are so many options that you'll have a hard time deciding. Natural colors are usually obtained from plants. For instance, spirulina imparts a green color to the soap. However, depending on the process you are using to create your soap, it can be a bright, vivid green or fade into a dull green. For example, while the green from spirulina looks stunning with M&P soaps, it's a dull green with CP soaps, mainly due to the saponification process.

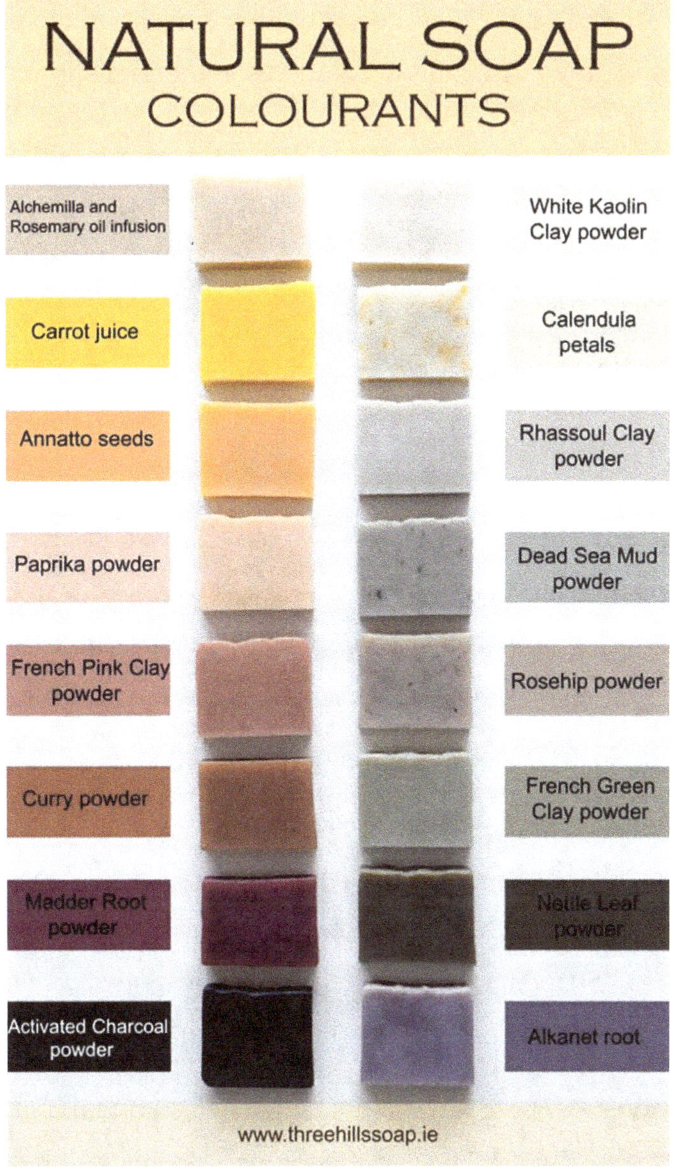

As you can see, you can choose to use different natural colorants for your soaps.

Clays are some of the best options if you're keen on using natural elements. Not only do they impart their beautiful colors, but they make the soap silky and add a slip you'll love when you use them! Additionally, the clay helps you relax and detoxify your body. A win-win situation!

Many soapers love using micas and oxides that are available naturally. However, some micas are mixed with other synthetic colors to create a new color, so they may not be entirely natural. You should check with your manufacturer to see how the mica was obtained.

Other natural colorants include activated charcoal, which is one of the most commonly used ingredients in soap making. Activated charcoal is also known to clear blemishes on your skin and have firming properties. And the natural, rich black color it imparts is amazing.

Synthetic colors – There are loads of synthetic colors available at your local craft store or online. Most of these colors are lab-made and beat the natural colorants by a mile in terms of vibrancy. Soapers obsessed with CP soaps tend to use synthetic colors because it makes the soap really stand out.

6) **Additives** – These are optional ingredients you add, depending on what you want the soap to look and smell like. Additives are common in both liquid and solid forms. Remember, colorful

soaps with no extra additives will work just as well, and some people love plain soaps with no colors, fragrances, or additives at all. It's just your preferences that matter here.

For example, dried lavender flowers are commonly used to add some character to the soap. Bear in mind that the additives don't necessarily add any value to the soap and are generally used for aesthetic purposes. However, some additives like sodium lactate, for example, are used to make the soap hard and firm.

Another common additive that soapers use is floral waters, otherwise known as hydrosols, to replace the distilled water in the recipe. Hydrosols are fragrant and do the job well, but it's just a waste of money in CP soap because the fragrance is lost in the harsh process. Don't forget that lye has a pH of 13, which will reduce the fragrance considerably. Even colorants tend to bleed out sometimes. That's why it's recommended that you add fragrances at the very last minute, just before pouring the batter into the mold.

Everything from aloe vera powder, orange peel powder, cranberry powder, rosebuds, and more are considered additives. Be careful about how you use them, though, because CP soaps tend to make the additives lose their colors. For instance, rosebuds mixed with the batter turn brown due to the high pH. However, they may be stable if they are sprinkled on top of the soap after it's poured into the mold.

Of course, extra additives mean extra money, so use them according to your budget. Keep in mind that a lot of additives can make the soap look crowded. Also, additives like dried flowers won't last after a couple of showers. Remember to use only dried items because fresh flowers and leaves will immediately lose their colors and look like blobs of brown stuck in the soap.

Chapter 4

Understanding the Soap Calculator

I mentioned a soap calculator in Chapter 1: Basics of Soap Making. This calculator, or any soap calculator, will be your holy grail for soap making. Even if you have a proven recipe in your hands, it always makes sense to quickly run the numbers for your satisfaction and safety.

SoapCalc is the most commonly used calculator for soapers. To make recipes, simply head on to http://soapcalc.net/calc/soapcalcwp.asp. And this is what you'll see:

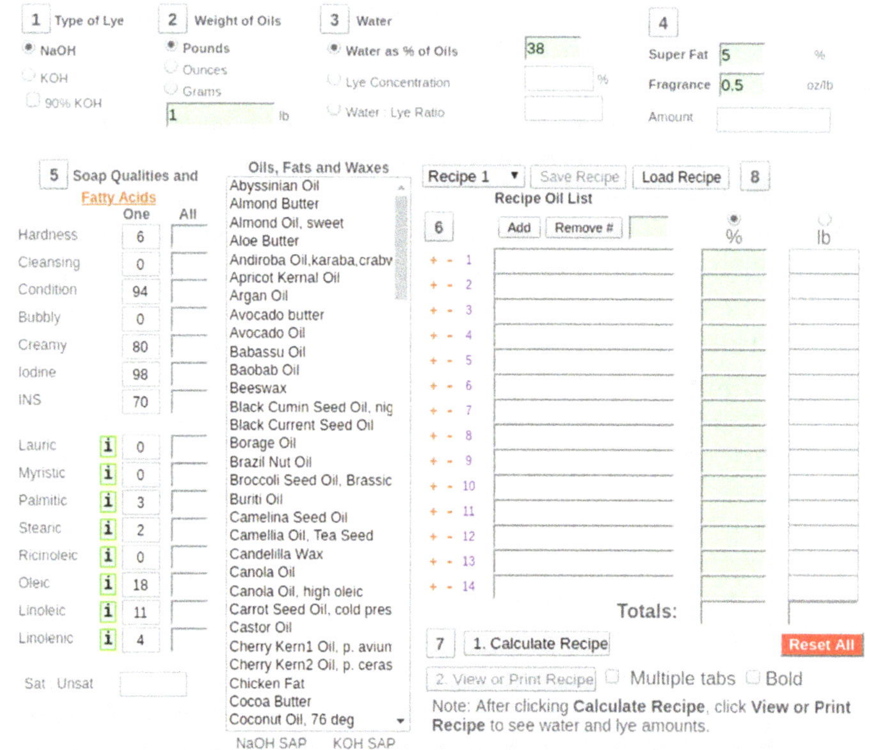

It's a simple calculator that allows you to make both solid (NaOH) and liquid (KOH) soap. For this book, though, we will focus only on solid bar recipes that use NaOH.

An overview of the calculator

Let's start at the very beginning. At the top left, you see:

1) Type of Lye

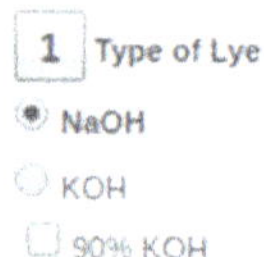

By default, SoapCalc has it set to NaOH (sodium hydroxide or lye). If you're making a solid bar of soap, leave it be.

2) Weight of Oils

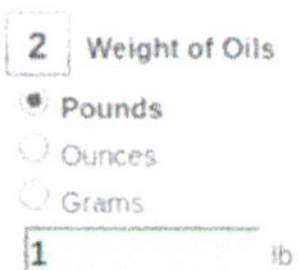

You can set it to grams, pounds, or ounces, depending on your preference.

3) Water

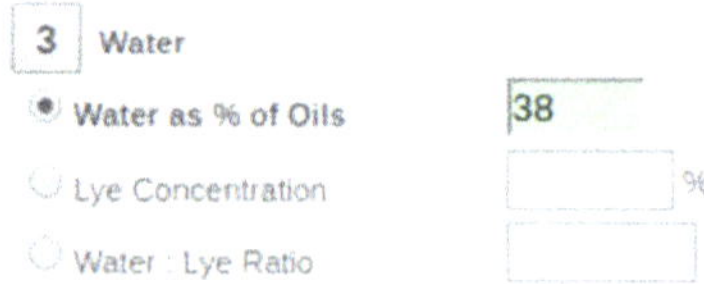

This section lets you adjust the water content of the recipe. Water is used to dissolve the lye. Through the process of making the soap, the water evaporates. At higher temperatures, more water is required, whereas less water is needed if soaping at lower temperatures.

Here, you can see the percentage of lye in a solution of lye and water. You can also use the "Water: Lye ratio," but I recommend that you use "Water as % of oils" at 38% as it's already set to avoid complications. Once you become an expert at soap-making, you can adjust the percentage to your liking.

For instance, experienced soapers sometimes like to set it at 33% since a reduction of water (a "water discount" as it's called will) decreases the amount of time needed to cure the soap. On the other end of the spectrum, it's best that you don't go above 40% since you'll end up with a messed-up soap. The more water there is, the safer the process becomes; however, too much water will leave you with soap that takes ages to cure! Therefore, I recommend that beginners stick to 38%.

For those who wish to water discount the recipe, be sure to keep an eye on the lye concentration. Anything above 40% lye concentration will speed up the chemical process and can produce certain surprising chemical reactions. Inexperienced soapers may be concerned if this happens, as the soap will bubble out or volcano out of the container you're using to make the soap. If you experience such a situation, run your spatula over the edges of the mixture rapidly to contain the mixture. As a preventative measure, it's a good idea to use a bigger container and thus avoid potential messes.

4) Super Fat

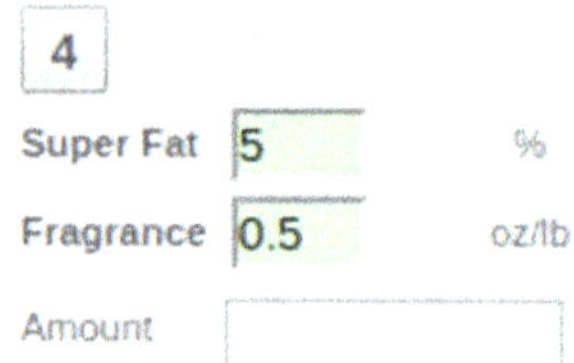

In the fourth section, you see something called "Super Fat." Super fat is nothing but the extra oil or fat your soap contains after the lye has reacted with the oils and the soap is completely saponified. For instance, you see a default setting of 5% super fat in the box. This is the oil that will not be saponified and floats in between soap molecules.

This oil (5% or whatever you choose) will deposit a very light layer of oil onto your skin. This doesn't mean that the soap doesn't cleanse. In fact, if you make soaps with no super fat at all, it can be VERY cleansing and dry up your skin a bit; the super fat will help keep your skin from drying out.

For example, using only coconut oil in your recipe produces hard bars of soap, but these bars can turn out to be much too dry. While some people prioritize the cleansing abilities of such a bar over a bar of soap with some super fat, they will be incredibly drying on the skin. Because 100% coconut oil soaps are so drying, they are typically used as laundry soaps rather than being used on the skin like 100% olive oil soaps, also known as castile soaps.

If, for some reason, you want to make a 100% coconut oil soap, you'll have to increase the super fat to at least 10-12% to reduce the dryness, which could turn out a little bit greasy. They are oils that float freely, after all. Thus, a combination of a cleansing oil like coconut would be ideally paired with a moisturizing oil such as olive oil.

If you're making soaps with soft oils and no super fat, it will still work, but you won't feel any softness at all, no matter what oil you use. For instance, if you use avocado oil for intense conditioning with no super fat in the soap, it will be no different than if you used any other oil because the lye will react to ALL the oils, and there will be no oil left over to condition your skin.

This means that you can't control which oil is saponified and which isn't. For example, if you make a bar of soap with 50% olive, 30% coconut, 10% rice bran, and 10% avocado, you can't expect the lye to react only to the coconut oil and allow the avocado to moisturize your skin. Some soapers believe that you can add your premium or luxurious oils at the end after trace when making CP soaps and consider that as super fat, but that's not how it works.

The lye will saponify every oil that it comes in contact with. This is a special concern with CP soaps because your batter will contain active lye even after it's poured into the mold. It will complete its saponification process in about 24-48 hours, and you will have no control over the oils. Thus, with CP soaps, just let the lye calculator do its job. It will subtract 5% from the oils so that you end up with a good moisturizing bar.

With Hot Process soaps, however, you have more control over the super fat. Yay! This means that you can use that avocado oil for moisturizing and be sure to benefit from it. For the calculations, you will set the super fat to 0 and let the calculator come up with the calculations. Then, you will use the total weight of your oils to come up with your free-floating super fat by yourself.

For example, if your total weight of oils is 10oz, simply multiply the number with the desired percentage of super fat:

10 oz X 0.05 (5%) = 0.5 oz

Your true total oil weight will be 10.5oz, of which 0.5 oz will be the free-floating superfat to be added last. Just when you're about to mold the soap, add the super fat, give it a good mix, and you're done!

5) Soap qualities and fatty acids

This is an important section if you want to design your soap in a specific manner based on desired characteristics. In other words, you get to tweak the moisturizing, hardness, or cleansing properties of the bar. A lot of soapers don't understand how this works. They often wonder why they end up with a slimy bar, soft bar, or even a super-hard bar, even when they have added moisturizing oils.

Well, the trick is to get a basic idea of the fatty acid profile of the oils, and you're golden. No, you don't have to call your old Chemistry professor! Just a basic idea is enough, and I'll show you how to go about it.

At first, you see this:

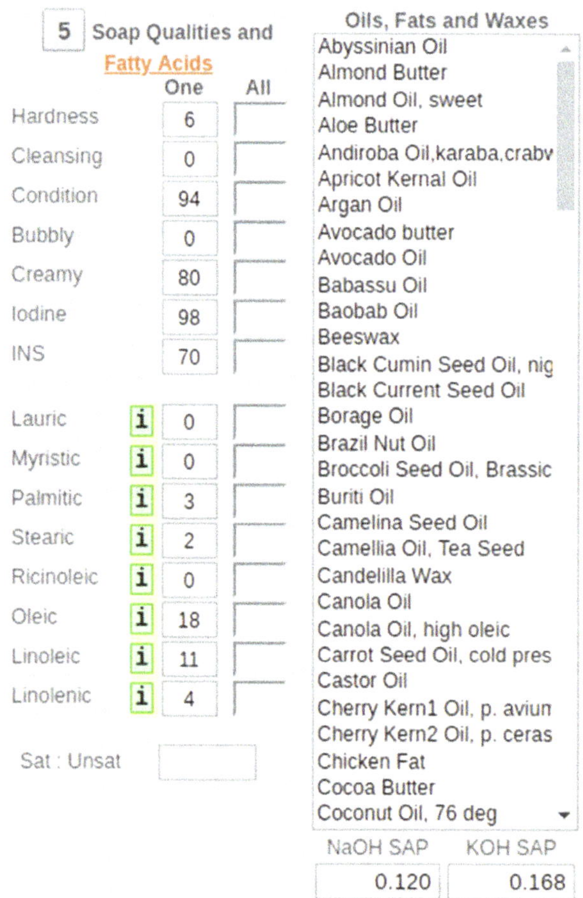

Let's go over what they all mean one by one.

Hardness

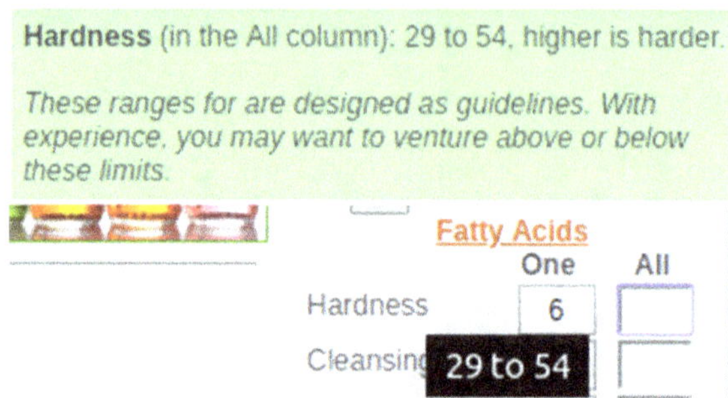

If you hover your mouse over the "Hardness" bar, you will see that SoapCalc considers anything in the range from 29 to 54 as satisfactory. Depending on how hard you want the soap to be, you can adjust the numbers. Generally speaking, the higher this number is, the harder the soap will be.

However, I have to tell you that the numbers can be deceptive at times. In fact, a soap's hardness primarily depends on the amount of water used in the recipe. Remember our mention of "water discount"? That's actually what determines the hardness.

Many soapers consider the number displayed in the "Hardness" section as the physical hardness of their soap. But the reality is that you can get a really hard bar of soap regardless of the oils you use if you adjust the water discount. Soaps will also become harder when they are cured for longer. Again, this is because the water evaporates as the soap cures.

You can check this by weighing a freshly cut soap and tracking its weight as it continues to cure. You will see that weight decreases as the soap cures and the water evaporates in the curing process.

Any soaper with some experience can attest to the fact that the "Hardness" on SoapCalc can be inaccurate. For instance, with a simple recipe for making a 100% olive oil soap cured for at least 4 weeks, you will end up with a rock-hard bar. Although the hardness number will show only 17, which is much less than SoapCalc's recommended minimum of 29, you will have a beautiful, hard bar of soap.

On SoapCalc, the hardness number is actually the result of the total saturated fatty acids, including palmitic, lauric, stearic, and myristic acids present in the oil. Since olive oil's fatty acids total to 17, the hardness number will make you think that you will get a soft bar. The reality, though, is that 100% olive oil soaps or castile soaps can produce some of the hardest bars of soaps. Keep this in mind while formulating a recipe, and you will only get better with time.

Cleansing

Next in line is "Cleansing". And you see that SoapCalc considers anything from 12 to 22 as a cleansing bar.

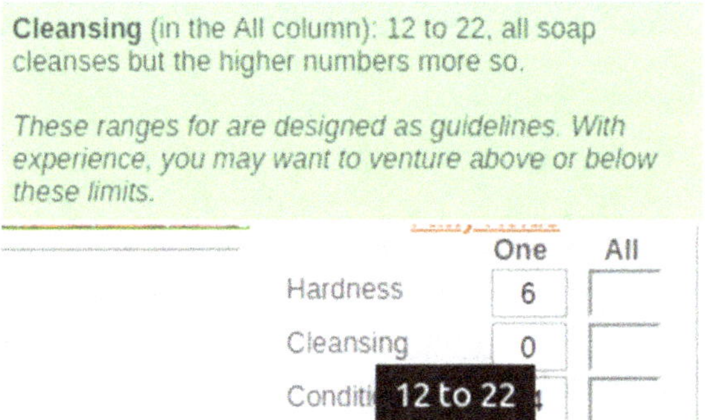

The higher the number, the better the cleansing properties, according to SoapCalc. This number refers to the ability of the soap to grab oils. The number is the total of the myristic and lauric percentages of the oils you choose.

While this number projects a pretty accurate description of the cleansing properties, keep in mind that the numbers for castile soap again shows that it's 0! So, does that mean that castile soap doesn't cleanse at all? Not at all! This means that it's less drying or stripping than other oils used in soap making.

On the other hand, it shows that the cleansing number is 67 for a 100% coconut oil soap, a number well above SoapCalc's recommended range of 12-22. To counter this problem, you can adjust the super fat to 15-20% and still get a good bar that's both hard and cleansing but moisturizes your skin. Keep in mind that SoapCalc doesn't consider the super fat when calculating the cleansing numbers, and that's why your oil's fatty acid profile should be considered.

Conditioning

Next, you see SoapCalc's numbers for Conditioning.

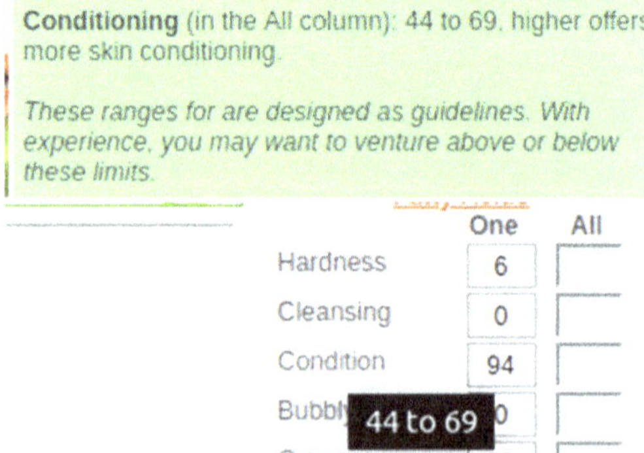

Here, SoapCalc mentions that the numbers refer to the emollient content of the soap. In general, the emollients will help your skin retain moisture. They also keep the skin super soft and silky. A range between 44-69 is decent enough, according to SoapCalc.

Remember that the fatty acids, including linoleic, oleic, linolenic, and ricinoleic acids, are added to get to the conditioning number you see here. While this is a reasonable approach, it doesn't completely accurately depict the full conditioning potential of your soap because it doesn't take the super fat into account.

In other words, remember that soap with 0% super fat will not moisturize your skin no matter what oils you use. Conversely, a soap with at least 5-10% super fat will feel silky and keep your skin soft.

Bubbly

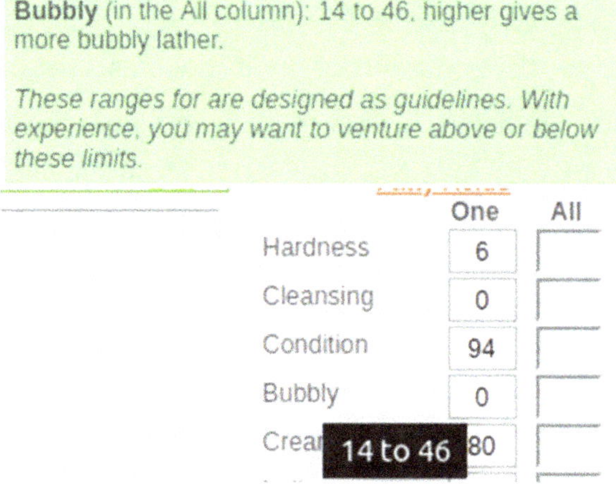

SoapCalc suggests that a range between 14 to 46 is ideal to produce a bubbly lather. The higher this number is, the more bubbles will be achieved. One way to increase the lather of a soap is to add sugar-containing ingredients like sugar solution, sorbitol, beer, or milk. Most soapers rely on castor oil to produce big bubbles, but coconut oil will also do the job just fine.

Creamy

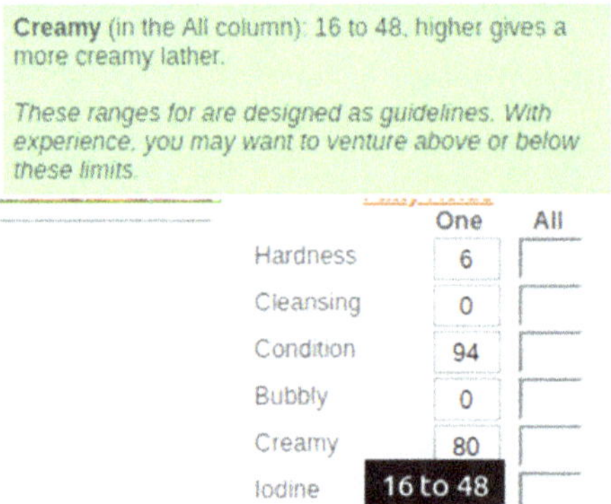

As you can see, anything in the range of 16-48 will ensure that the soap's lather is creamier. Remember that if you want a bubblier lather, the creaminess will decrease and vice versa. Again, the fatty acids are added to get the value. Since fatty acids like stearic acid and palmitic acid produce great lather, you can include oils that produce such fatty acids.

By now, you hopefully have a clearer understanding of how SoapCalc works and how the numbers can be tweaked to suit your needs. Don't bother with the Iodine or the INS. Next, we will discuss selecting the oils to create great yet simple recipes that produce amazing soaps.

Chapter 5

How to Make Cold Process Soap

Many people wonder if they can make soap without lye. So many, in fact, that it is a common search term on Google. The short answer is no. You can't make soap without lye. However, what you can do instead is use pre-made bases where the saponification has already occurred, as with Melt and Pour soaps. If you want to make soap from scratch, you have to handle lye. But you can avoid using lye if you're using pre-made bases available in your local market and online. Remember that the final product does NOT contain lye. Once the saponification process is complete, all traces of lye disappear.

If you're okay with handling lye and really want to make soap from scratch, read on...

As mentioned already, CP soap is the result of a chemical reaction that occurs when an alkali like lye and fats such as oil or butter react with each other. In this process, the lye is neutralized without the intervention of outside sources like heat. And since there's no heat, it takes more time to cure than other processes. Additionally, the lack of heat allows the soap to preserve more of the beneficial attributes of the oil you've used. So, in simple terms, CP creates some of the best soaps but definitely requires more patience.

Once you measure out the oils, lye, and water, you can combine them all using your blender or mix them tediously by hand. But before pouring them into the molds, they need to be brought to trace. "Now, what in the world is trace?" you ask.

Trace

Trace is nothing but a thorough mixture of all ingredients used to make soap (oil, water, and lye). You now know that the saponification process begins once you start mixing these ingredients together. If the ingredients all mix and blend well together, they will not separate, but if they do, you'll have problems!

When you combine the ingredients by using a blender or by hand, they will begin to combine together and turn milky. As you mix them further, the mixture becomes creamier. This process is called emulsification and is the process of mixing two liquids that are normally un-mixable, such as oil and water. Soapers refer to this as "Trace."

There are three different stages of trace that can be reached, and it all depends on the type of soap and the design you want to achieve, as well as which one you should choose.

Thin trace

Once you begin soaping, you'll notice that the mixture of ingredients thickens with time, by which I mean that it thickens within 5-10 minutes. As soon as the lye, oils, and water combine, they look like pancake batter. If there are no oil streaks left behind, then you know that the ingredients have emulsified.

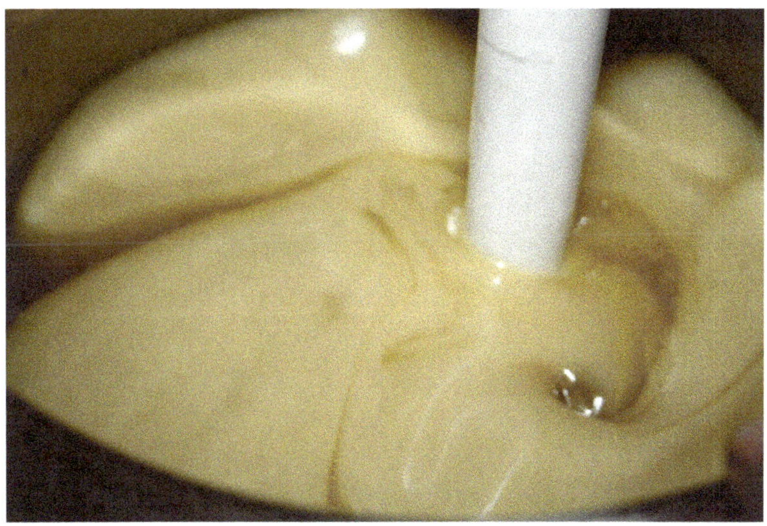

In this picture, you can see oil pooling at the top. That means that it hasn't reached trace yet. You continue to blend.

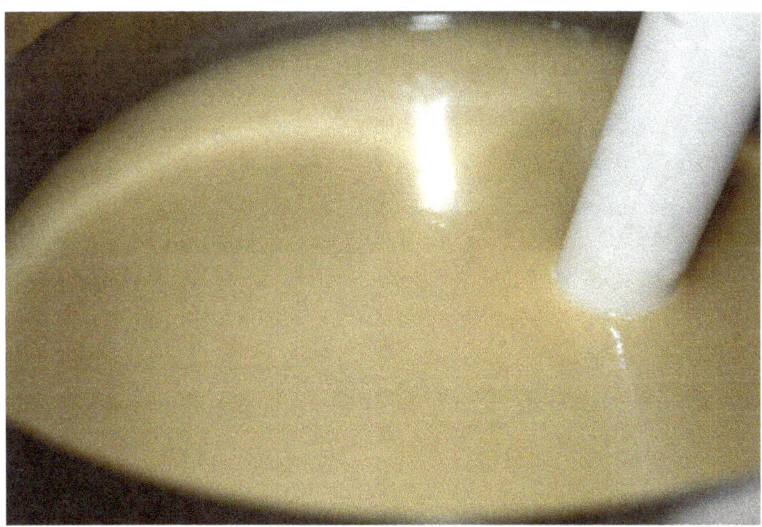

Here, the emulsification is complete, and you don't see oil floating at the top. Thin trace refers to soap batter that's combined well but is still easy to pour. Soapers prefer thin traces to create designs that need a lot of swirling. It's easier to create any design you want as long as the batter is thin and easy to pour.

Medium Trace

As you combine the mixture a little more, you'll see that it becomes thicker. It now looks more like cake batter. I add my colors at this stage so that it mixes well. An easy way to recognize medium trace is to drizzle the batter back on the batter itself (yes, you read that right!).

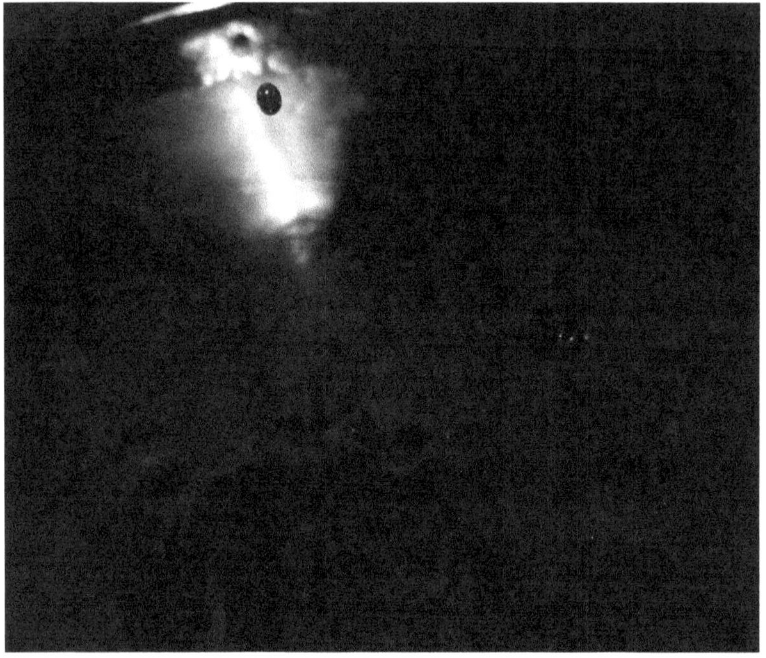

If you notice little drops or trails where the batter is drizzled, it's medium trace. If not, it's a thin trace. Medium trace is best if you want the soap to cure faster.

Thick Trace

If you continue mixing past when the soap reaches medium trace, it continues becoming thicker and thicker. In fact, it becomes so thick that you'll have to spoon it onto the mold. Naturally, this thicker soap will cure faster. Soapers love to create thick traces so they can use them to create designs on the tops. For instance, you can make normal soap and spoon out thick trace soap as toppings to make it look like ice cream! Or maybe even pudding. It totally depends on what you want to make.

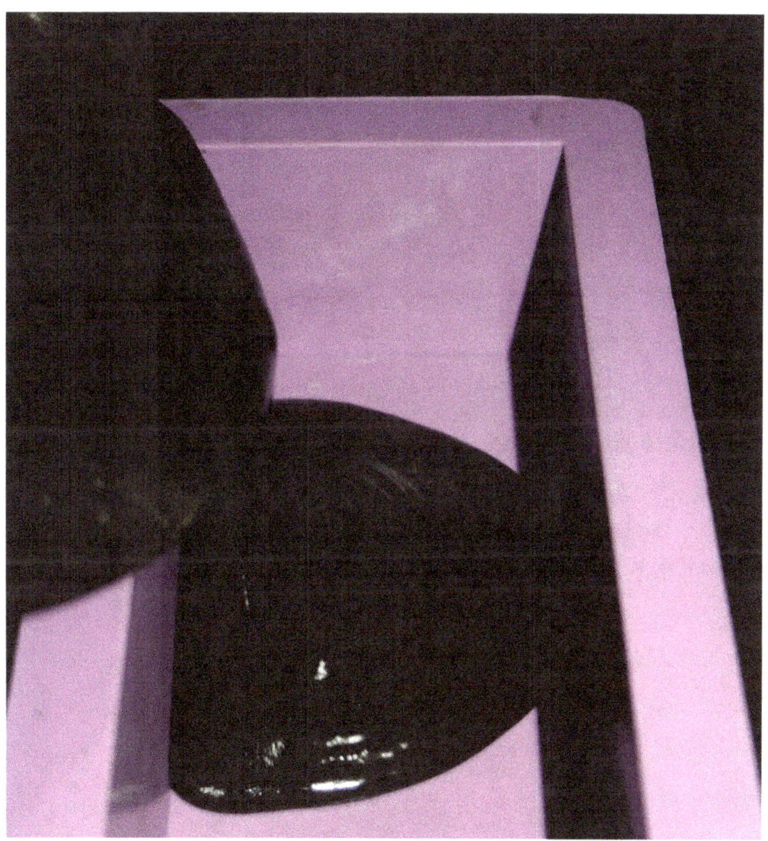

In this picture, the batter is thick already. It's somewhere between medium to thick trace. Once you've reached the desired thickness, that's when you pour it into the mold. Once the batter has been poured into the mold, it may take anywhere from 2 to 3 days for it to be ready to unmold, depending on the water content, super fat, and any number of additional factors. Usually, the soap completes the saponification process in about 24 hours. However, you cannot use it right away since it needs to cure.

Curing is extremely important because it's when the lye is slowly used up while the water evaporates. And that's exactly why soaps with less water cure faster. To understand how this works, try weighing the soap as soon as you cut it. Then let it cure. Weigh the soap at least once every week, and you'll notice that the weight will decrease as time goes on. It's nothing but the water evaporating!

Do not ever use CP soap directly as soon as you cut it. Although a lot of the lye is used up within 24 hours, the soap will still be lye-heavy, and you'd never want to use that. As the soap cures, it transforms into a hard bar that lasts a long while and no longer contains lye.

So, now that you have gotten the gist of the process let's dive into it!

For this example, I'll be making an activated charcoal CP soap. I have chosen a very simple recipe to ensure that you don't find it too complicated.

I only need olive oil, coconut oil, and castor oil to make a splendid bar of soap. You can tweak this recipe, but make sure you run it on SoapCalc before proceeding. Here's a simple recipe that makes 1.5 pounds or 700 grams of soap.

Olive oil pomace – 317.5 grams

Coconut oil – 113.40 grams

Castor oil – 22.68 grams

Distilled water – 149.69 grams

Lye – 62.94 grams

Sodium lactate – 1.5 teaspoons

Activated charcoal – 3 tbsp

Black Mica – 1 tbsp

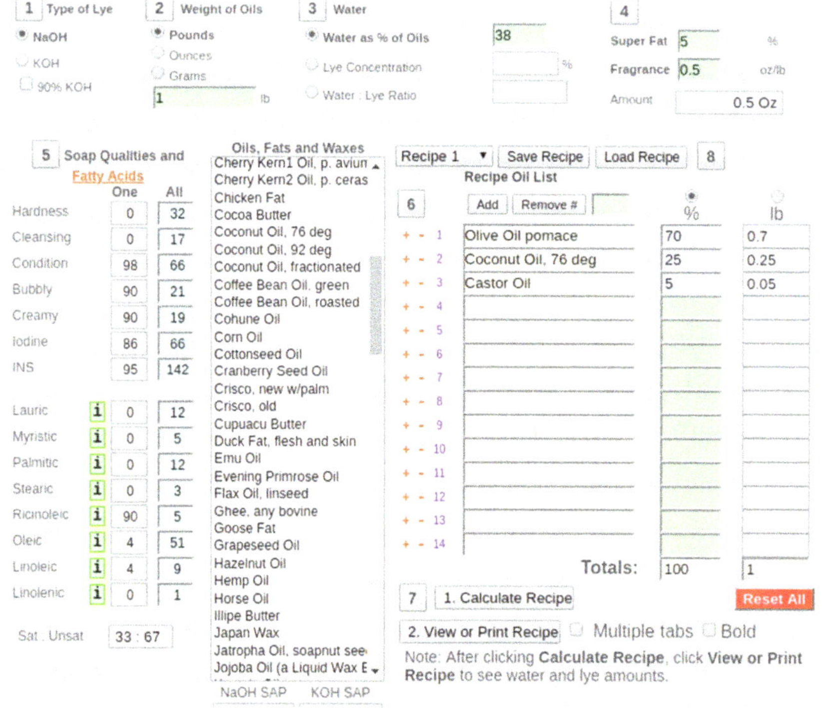

SoapCalc ©	Recipe Name:				New INCI Names Print Recipe

Total oil weight	1 lb	Sat : Unsat Ratio	33 : 67
Water as percent of oil weight	**38.00 %**	Iodine	66
Super Fat/Discount	5 %	INS	142
Lye Concentration	26.748 %	Fragrance Ratio	0.5
Water : Lye Ratio	2.7386:1	Fragrance Weight	0.50 oz

	Pounds	Ounces	Grams
Water	0.380	6.08	172.36
Lye - NaOH	0.139	2.22	62.94
Oils	1.000	16.00	453.59
Fragrance	0.031	0.50	14.18
Soap weight before CP cure or HP cook	1.550	24.80	703.07

#	√	Oil/Fat	%	Pounds	Ounces	Grams
1		Olive Oil pomace	70.00	0.700	11.20	317.51
2		Coconut Oil, 76 deg	25.00	0.250	4.00	113.40
3		Castor Oil	5.00	0.050	0.80	22.68
		Totals	100.00	1.000	16.00	453.59

Soap Bar Quality	Range	Your Recipe		
Hardness	29 - 54	32	Lauric	12
Cleansing	12 - 22	17	Myristic	5
Conditioning	44 - 69	66	Palmitic	12
Bubbly	14 - 46	21	Stearic	3
Creamy	16 - 48	19	Ricinoleic	5
Iodine	41 - 70	66	Oleic	51
INS	136 - 165	142	Linoleic	9
			Linolenic	1

Additives	Notes
Sodium lactate – 1.5 teaspoons Activated charcoal – 3 tbsp Black Mica – 1 tbsp	

To begin making the recipe, follow these step-by-step instructions:

1) Prepare your work area

Although soap-making is an amazing and rewarding endeavor, it can be dangerous if you don't do it in a safe work area, both for you and those whom you share space with. Not everyone has the luxury of working in their basement or getting a manufacturing unit, but the least you can do is work in an area that's not accessible to children and pets and has a free flow of air.

You need to select an area that has access to a sink and a heating source. Although you won't need to cook the batter if you're making Cold Process soap, you'll still need to heat the oils, so having a microwave or other heating source will certainly help you. It is also very important that there is a free flow of fresh air, as the lye mixture will be giving off fumes that should *not* be breathed in. It is best to work with an open window or ventilating system.

If you're worried about damaging your countertop, cover it with newspaper or a similar protective cover to catch any spills that occur. And trust me, you will see some spillage in the process.

2) Equip yourself properly

I have already spoken about the dangers of soap-making without using any safety measures, but I'll do it again because it is incredibly important. You must remember that lye is as dangerous as acid, and it really hurts. If you come into contact with the lye, rinse the area with plain, cool water for several minutes. Some people suggest applying vinegar on areas of the skin that come in contact with lye to neutralize it, but I don't recommend doing so. The vinegar will neutralize the lye, but the difference in pH is too much for your skin to bear and may actually cause additional trauma to the affected area. Plain water will suffice.

To avoid burns, cover as much of your skin as possible with long sleeves and pants. You should also wear your gloves and goggles until you pour the soap into the mold and have safely stored it.

3) Measure water

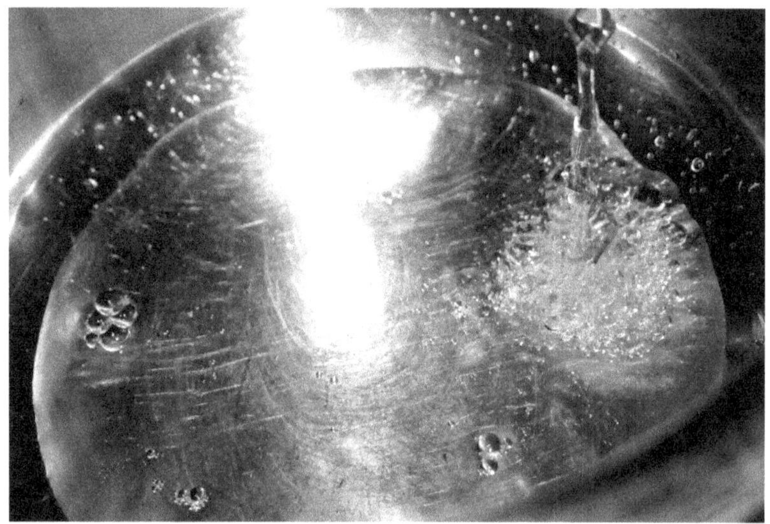

Measure the distilled water. If you're changing anything in this recipe, make sure you check your recipe on SoapCalc again. Seriously, I can't stress this enough.

4) Measure out the oils

No matter what recipe you intend to make, ensure you have the recipe in front of you before you begin. This reduces guesswork and makes the process go much smoother. Also, start with small batches, especially when you're a beginner, to reduce possible waste while you are learning. It also makes sense to stick to simple oils rather than overcomplicating the recipe by adding way too many different types of oils.

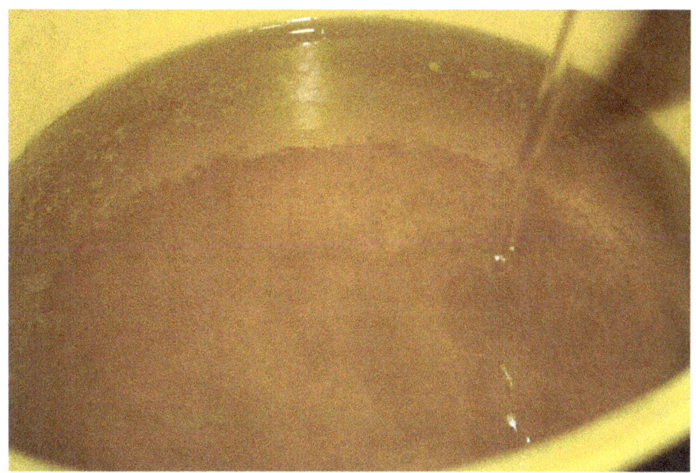

There are only three oils in this particular recipe. Note that this recipe yields a small batch of soap, so you won't waste too much if something goes wrong. However, if you follow the instructions and measure everything by weight, you'll be fine.

Now, after making the lye solution, it's time to measure the oils. For this recipe, measure Coconut oil and Olive oil in a microwave-safe container. Do it one by one, but don't forget to tare the scale (set to zero with your empty measuring container on the scale) every time you measure a particular oil, or you'll be confused.

Heat up your oils using a microwave or on a stovetop. If you use a microwave, use small intervals of 30-60 seconds to heat up your oils, or you'll risk burning them! Some people love using steel containers, even for their oils, but these obviously can't be microwaved. If you intend to use steel containers, heat the oils up on the stove, but be sure to keep an eye on them.

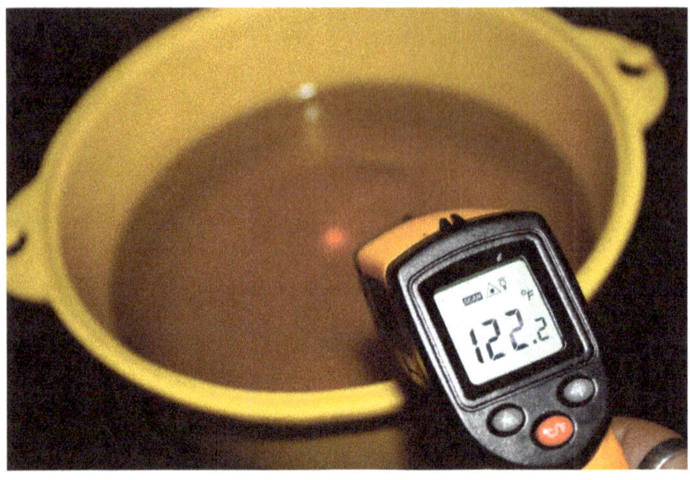

Temperature plays a very important role in soap making, particularly when dealing with the oils. Most soapers prefer somewhere in the range of 120-130 ° F. This means that both the lye solution and oil should be within about 10 degrees of this range. Soapers that love this range do because it ensures that the oils and butter are completely melted. Other soapers prefer a range of 100-110 ° F, and it still works fine. Just remember that if you stray too far from the recommended temperatures, some common problems will occur.

If you soap when oils have cooled too much, they will produce a false trace. Now you understand that trace means emulsification of your soap, but a false trace will make you think that the mixture has been thoroughly emulsified even when it hasn't! If the lye solution is too cold, it will force the oils to solidify upon contact. Conversely, if the lye solution is too hot, it heats the soap so much that it volcanoes out of the mold. This is why you must keep an eye on the temperature at all times.

5) Measure lye

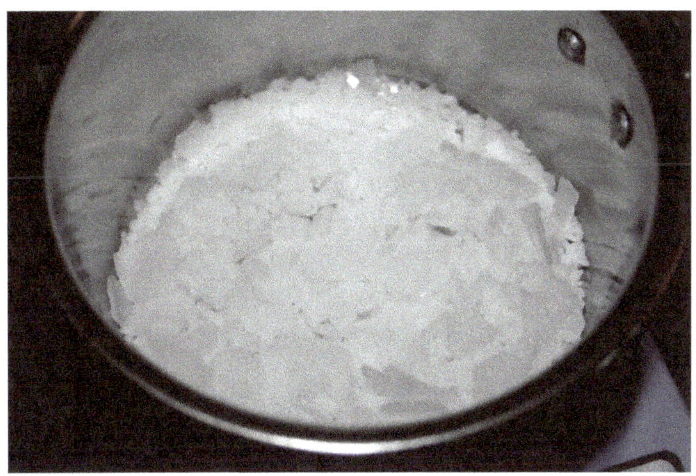

Make sure you do this *after* weighing your water and oils. Why? Well, lye – sodium hydroxide – tends to absorb water from the air. In a matter of a few minutes, you'll notice that it becomes watery. Thus, you should work quickly at this point.

6) Prepare lye water solution

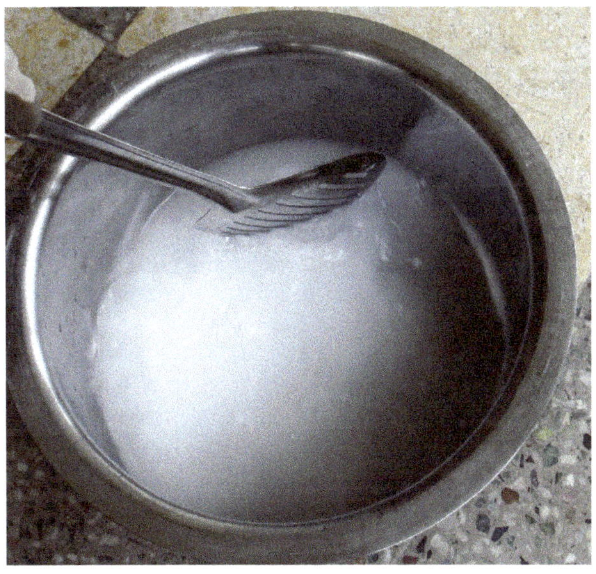

In order to make the lye solution, use a stainless-steel container. Glass can break, and plastic can melt if it's not resistant enough, so steel is the best option. Keep your scales clean and ready to weigh the ingredients.

Place your empty steel container on top of the scale. This gives you the weight of your container, but you don't need that, so remember to press "tare" on your scale to bring it to zero. Now, pour the lye into the container to measure it. Remember, you should have measured the oils and water already, so measuring the lye should be the last measurement you take.

After you have measured the lye, pour the water into the lye. NEVER POUR LYE INTO WATER! Always remember to pour the water into the lye. I remember this as L to W, like the order of the alphabet, but you can remember it any way you want. Also, mix the lye a little at a time to prevent issues.

Now, begin mixing with a spatula. The water will look cloudy, and the container will become very hot – often reaching 200°F – but mix it as best as you can. It's also important not to inhale the fumes, which is why it's best to work in open areas. If that's not possible, open the windows to prevent inhaling fumes.

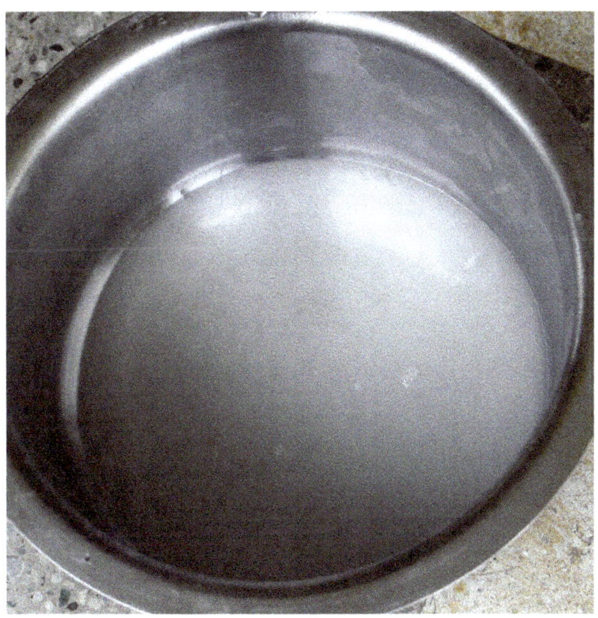

Stir the solution thoroughly until all the lye disappears. The solution will still look milky, but you can set it aside and wait for it to cool down. This is the point at which you should add the sodium lactate.

But what happens if you pour lye into water, you ask? It's the same thing, right? Wrong! Though the chemicals are the same, the reaction will occur differently. When you pour water into a container with lye, the water begins dissolving the lye immediately to form a crust. A lot of reactions occur beneath this crust, and the end result is an eruption resembling a volcano. It's also known as the volcano effect because it bursts quite violently and can harm you if it touches you.

If you ever make the mistake of pouring water on lye, make sure everything's calm before you get to work. Wipe all surfaces soaked with lye with soapy water to remove the lye. You can also spray vinegar on all surfaces to neutralize the alkali before wiping.

7) Measure out the remaining ingredients

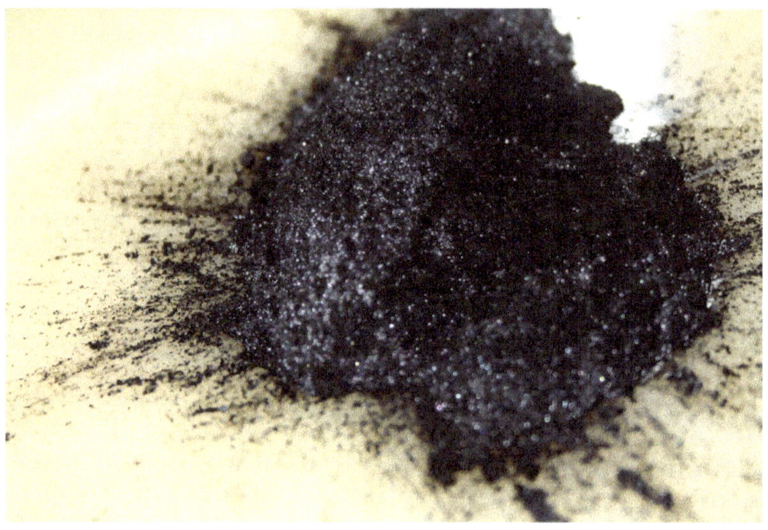

While you're waiting for the lye solution and oils to cool down to the correct temperature to be mixed, you can weigh your other ingredients, including fragrance oils. Also, get your glitters, colors, and other additives like sodium lactate ready to use before proceeding. Prepare the mold by wiping it clean and dry.

8) Making the soap

Yay! So, we are finally at this stage. So, once you've measured the oils and lye solution and are satisfied with the temperature, you can now start making the soap. Before you begin, ensure that you have everything ready to go on the workstation. And *don't* forget your safety equipment! You should still be wearing it from preparing the lye solution!

We now have the lye solution, which has cooled down considerably, and the oils in front of us. Start by pouring the lye solution into the oils, though it doesn't really matter if you pour the oils into the solution. This process does not hold the same risks as creating your lye solution.

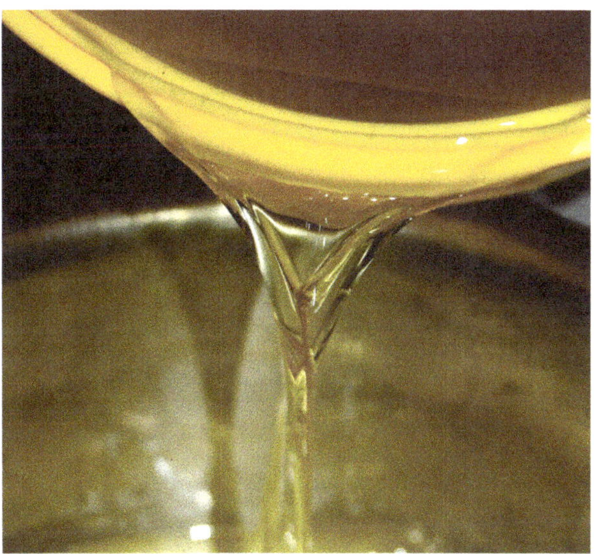

Grab a spatula and give it a quick stir. If you prefer making soap by mixing with just your hands, I'll warn you that it will take a lot of time. Then, continue to mix.

If you, like most other soapers, prefer a stick blender, now's the time to start combining the oils and lye thoroughly. Immerse the blender completely in the batter so you don't risk any spills. Make sure you give it 2-3 quick stirs and stop;

going all out with the stick blender will make the batter super thick very fast.

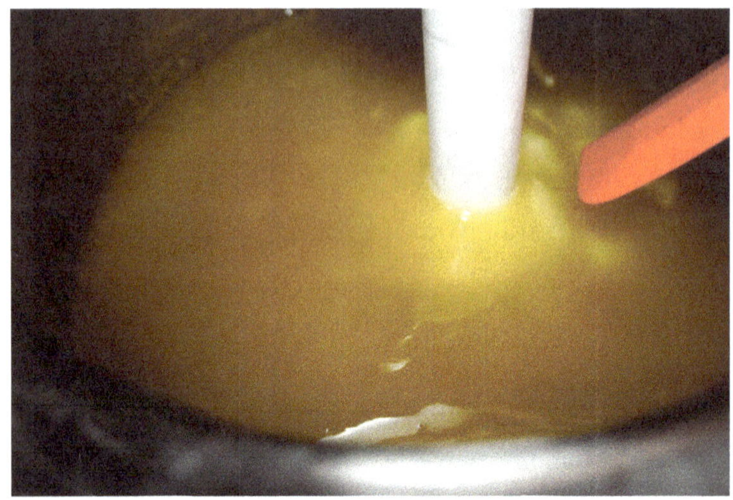

Continue stirring and incorporating the ingredients using bursts. The oils will pool at the top when you begin, but as you continue mixing, you'll see that the solution slowly changes color. What starts as a cloudy mixture will become more and more opaque as you continue.

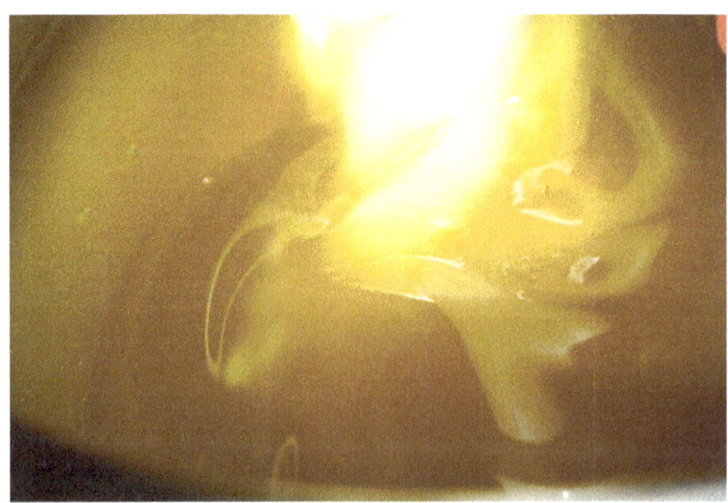

Use the spatula to scrape down the sides while the stick blender rests in the batter. A few quick bursts later, you should reach a thin trace. But then again, it depends on the type of oils you've used and how quickly you'll reach trace.

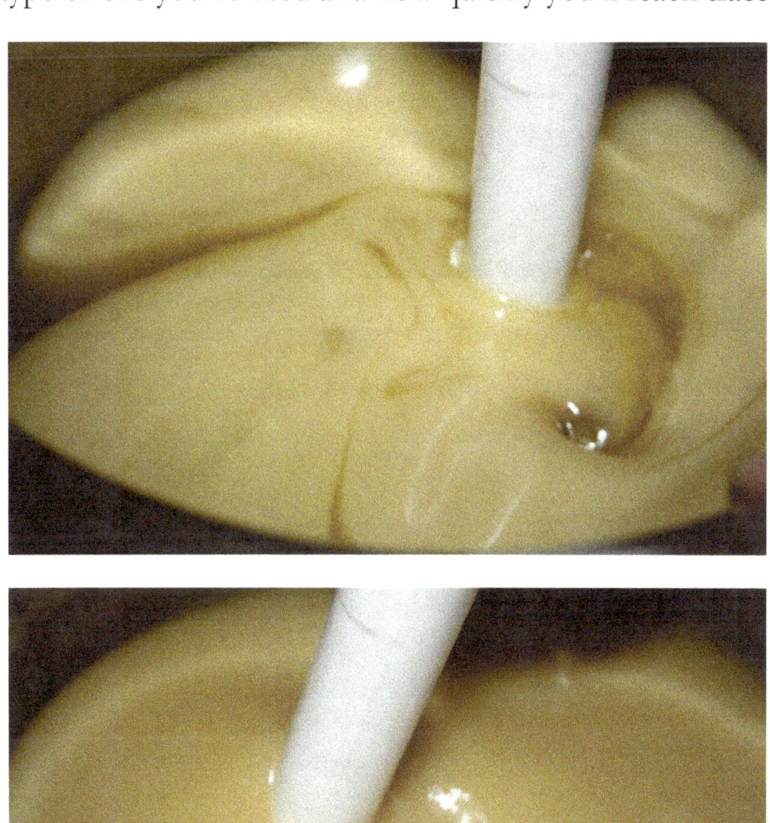

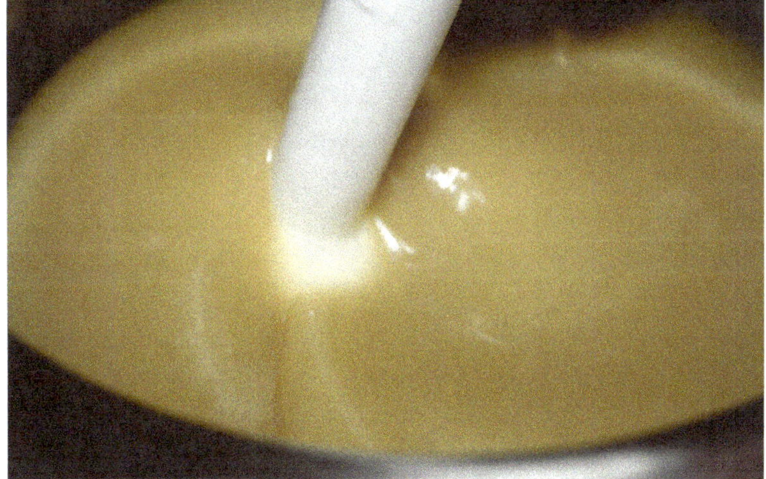

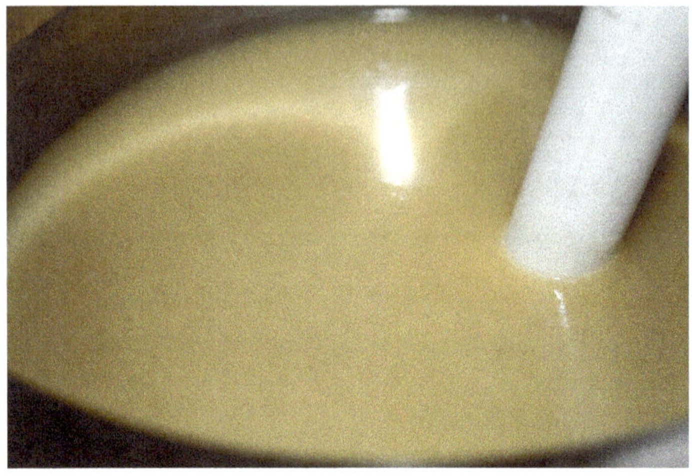

For instance, if you've used a large percentage of olive oil, it will take a longer time to reach trace whereas a soap dominated by coconut oil will reach trace fairly quickly. Drizzle the batter back on itself to check for trace. It must be thin enough to pour, but it should also leave traces on the top. As you know, if it has reached trace, then that means that the soap has saponified.

9) Add additives

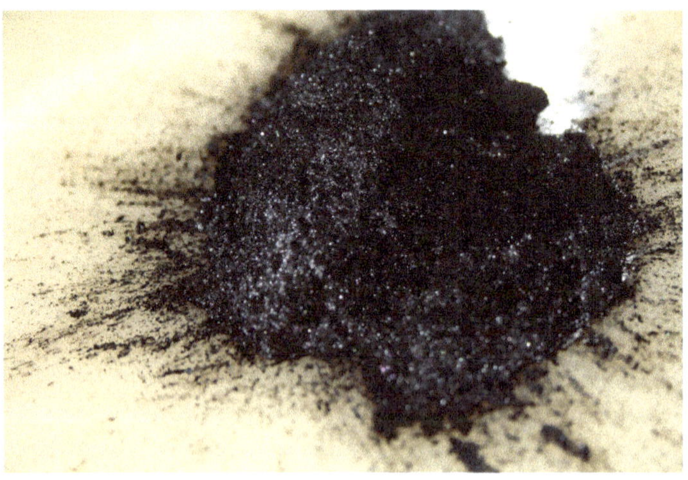

Apart from the sodium lactate that was added to the lye water solution at the very beginning, put in all of your other additives, like colors and fragrances, while the batter is still at a thin trace. If you wait for it to thicken too much, the colors will not mix properly. You should also account for the batter thickening throughout this addition, as you'll be using the blender to mix the colors and fragrances, and the blending process will naturally thicken the batter.

Therefore, it's best to add colors, fragrances, and any other additives (such as the activated charcoal and black mica in this recipe) when the mixture is at a thin trace. Personally, I prefer adding my colors to the oils much before I begin stick blending. I choose to do this because I don't have to worry about the batter thickening with every single burst of the blender and it also gives me more time and control. I also add my fragrances at the very end so they won't lose all of their potency.

Once all of your additives are incorporated, give the batter a final, quick stir.

10) Pour the soap into the mold

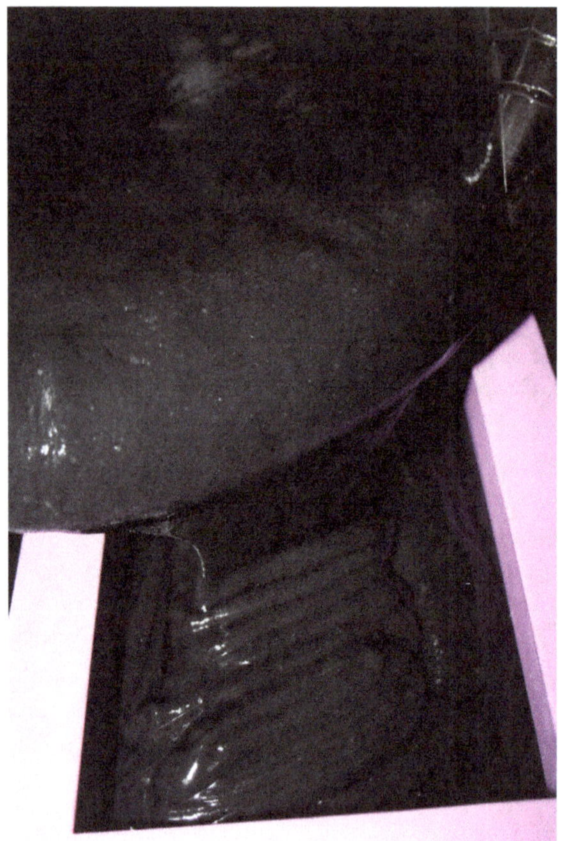

Grab the pot or container with the soap batter and pour it slowly into the mold. This recipe is pretty basic and doesn't show you any complicated designs, but as you gain more experience, I'm sure that you'll be creating lots of designs in your soaps. From using dividers to swirling with a hanger to even creating picturesque scenes on the soap, there are lots of designs to incorporate as you gain skills!

Once you finish pouring, scrape any remaining soap batter out of the container with a spatula. You can also add any glitter or other external toppings, like dried flowers, that you like to make the soap look pretty. Finally, tap the mold firmly, but without splattering, on a hard surface to remove any air bubbles. Alternatively, you can spray some isopropyl alcohol on the surface of the wet soap to remove the air bubbles.

11) Set the soap aside

Even after you're done pouring the soap, you can influence the outcome. For example, if you wrap the mold with a towel and ensure that it stays warm for a while, the soap will be forced to gel, making the colors look more vivid. You can also achieve this effect by sticking the mold into an oven with just the lights on. Don't bake the soap, though!

However, if you love soap without a gelled look like the one I have here, simply place it in a safe place that isn't too warm. You can also place it in the fridge to be sure that it doesn't gel, but that's not really required.

12) Unmold the soap

Most recipes will take about a day for it to be ready to be unmolded. But waiting for 2-3 days isn't unheard of. In fact, castile soaps take up to a week due to all that olive oil! So, once you're sure that the soap has hardened enough, unmold the soap and cut it into bars using a knife. You get professional soap cutters, but you should only invest in them only if you love making soap. You can also use cheese cutters that work exactly like soap cutters!

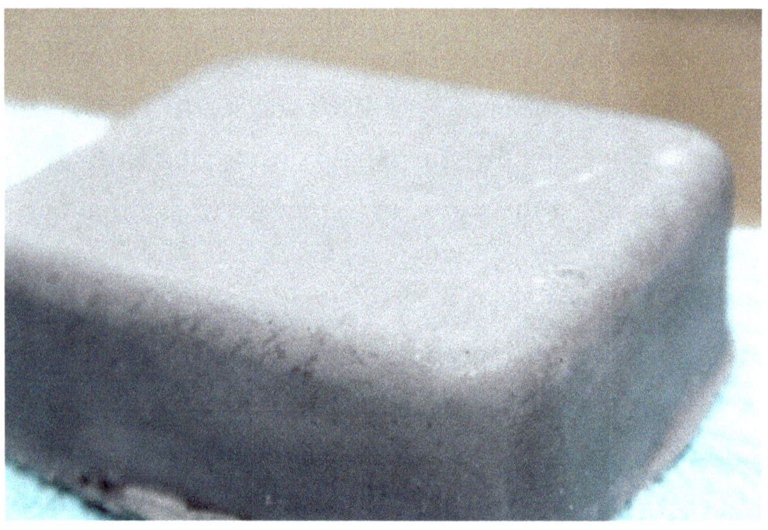

13) Cure the soap

Do not ignore this step, as it is the most important part of the process. Unless you're okay with using lye-heavy soaps that itch and irritate your skin, make sure you place your soaps in a place with great ventilation for at least 4-6 weeks. The longer the soaps cure, the harder they will become.

Many people come up with creative ways to cure their soaps, including curing them on shoe stands. Of course, make sure that the area is clean before you begin curing the soaps. Also, note that you shouldn't place the soaps in sunlight to cure, but there should be a lot of airflow to help them cure. Wooden or steel racks work well for this. Some soapers use laundry bags with several layers because they can also work amazingly well for curing soaps.

And that's it! You've just made some stunning Cold Process soap! Remember that you can tweak this recipe to your heart's content but try not to change the values of water discount too much until you've gained some experience. The best way to ensure that you get a hard bar of soap is to stick to 33-38%. The more lye you add, the harder and quicker it sets, whereas the more water you add, the longer it will take.

Notice that the soap looks grey rather than black. You can increase the amount of activated charcoal to get jet-black soaps. Also, there will be a white layer on the soaps as they are cured. That's because of soda ash that is naturally deposited on the soaps. To solve the problem, you can simply apply hot steam on the soaps and then let them cure again.

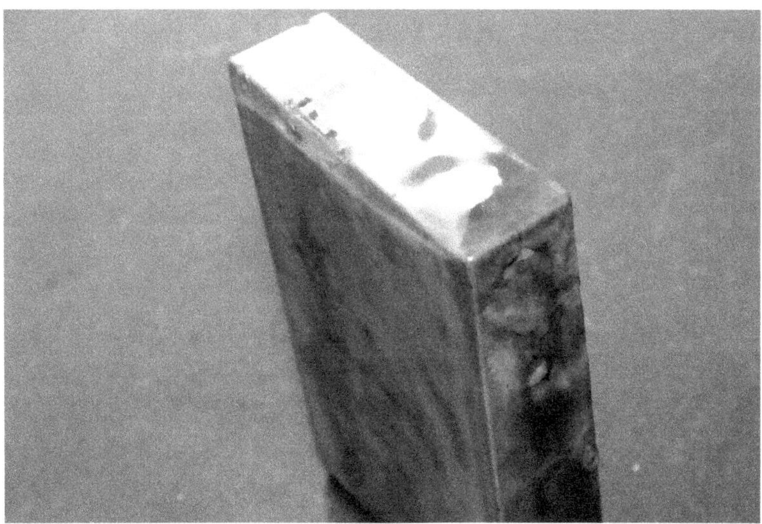

Once you've gotten rid of the soda ash, let it sit and dry.

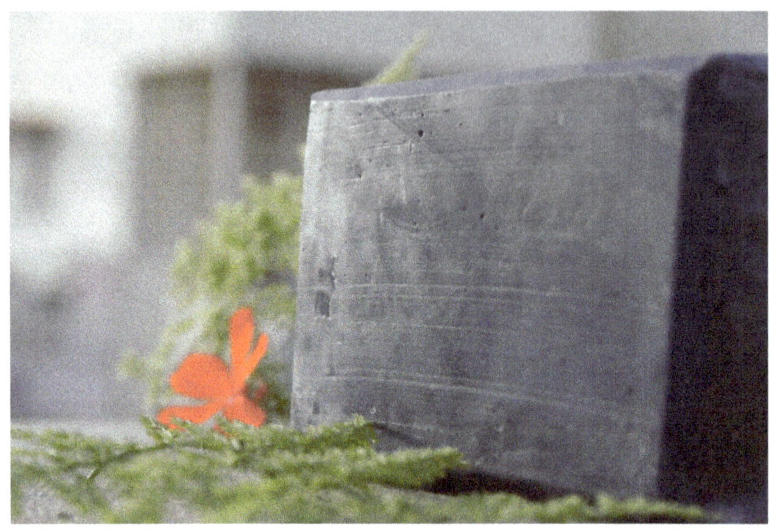

Superfat doesn't make a lot of difference in CP soaps. As mentioned earlier, the lye eats up whatever oils it interacts with indiscriminately and doesn't care about whether you've used a premium or ordinary oil if you wish to customize the recipe where you can enjoy lathering yourself with soaps containing oils you've specifically picked, move on to Hot Process soap.

Chapter 6

How to Create Recipes

So, now that you have a basic understanding of the types of ingredients that can be used, it's important to understand how to use them in your own recipes. You'll be able to create any kind of soap with experience. However, if you don't learn to apply your knowledge, you'll be forced to follow other recipes all your life. It's not complicated, really, so let's get it over with.

First, we must go over the different types of recipes you can make. For that, recollect the guidelines mentioned in Chapter 2. Remember that the recipe you consider the best may not work for everyone. Everyone's preferences for a soap will vary. You may like soap with a lot of lather, but someone else prefers creamier soap.

It's also important to formulate recipes that create hard bars of soap. Would you like a soap that gets used up within a week? No! What about something so hard that it lasts for ages but is nearly impossible to use? No, again! The trick is to strike a balance between these two extremes. And, of course, it shouldn't overshoot your budget.

Recipe for all types

I have mentioned this earlier, but we will go through this again to refresh your memory. There are strategies to make a firm bar of soap that lasts a long time. For instance, you can reduce the amount of water in the recipe. You can also add waxes, such as beeswax, in small amounts (2%) to the oils, but before you add the lye. Of course, adding salt or sodium lactate will work wonderfully, too. Although hard oils like coconut oils are preferred, soft oils like olive oil can also produce really hard bars. Other options include adding stearic acid at about 0.5% of the total oils to increase hardness.

Let's begin formulating by adding the base ingredients. To make sure that you get a hard bar, we'll start with a ratio of 50% hard oils and 50% soft oils.

Hard oils that are perfect for producing lather are babassu, palm, coconut, and all types of butter. Adding coconut at 60% of your hard oils will be all right. You can also add butter like Shea to get a nourishing bar. Adding some lard would also be fantastic.

For the softer oils, including olive oil, it is always a safe bet. It will take more time to cure, but the results are amazing, and it produces a creaminess you wouldn't believe. You could start by adding at least 20% of olive oil to your soft oil. For more lather, simply include castor oil at 6%, but don't go beyond 10% since it makes the bar slimy.

Recipe for a hard bar:

50% Hard Oils (a mixture of coconut oil, palm oil, shea butter, cocoa butter, tallow, and lard)

50% soft oils (olive oil, castor oil, avocado oil, and sweet almond oil)

For example, you could use:

20% Coconut oil

20% Palm oil

8% Cocoa Butter

2% Beeswax

0.5% Stearic acid

30% Olive oil

10% Sunflower oil

5% Castor oil

4.5% Sweet almond oil

1 teaspoon of Sodium lactate for every pound of oils

Now that you have the recipe, I'll show you how to calculate it using SoapCalc. Open <u>SoapCalc</u> and this is what you will see:

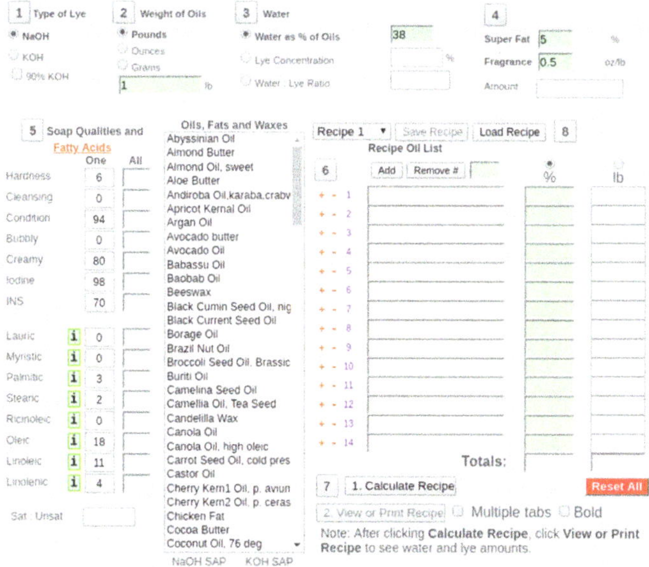

Now, we add the oils one by one, including the desired percentages. I usually use water discount at 33% for a hard bar, but remember that it will hit trace faster. To add the oils, click on any oil and click "Add" right below "Recipe Oil List."

And you get:

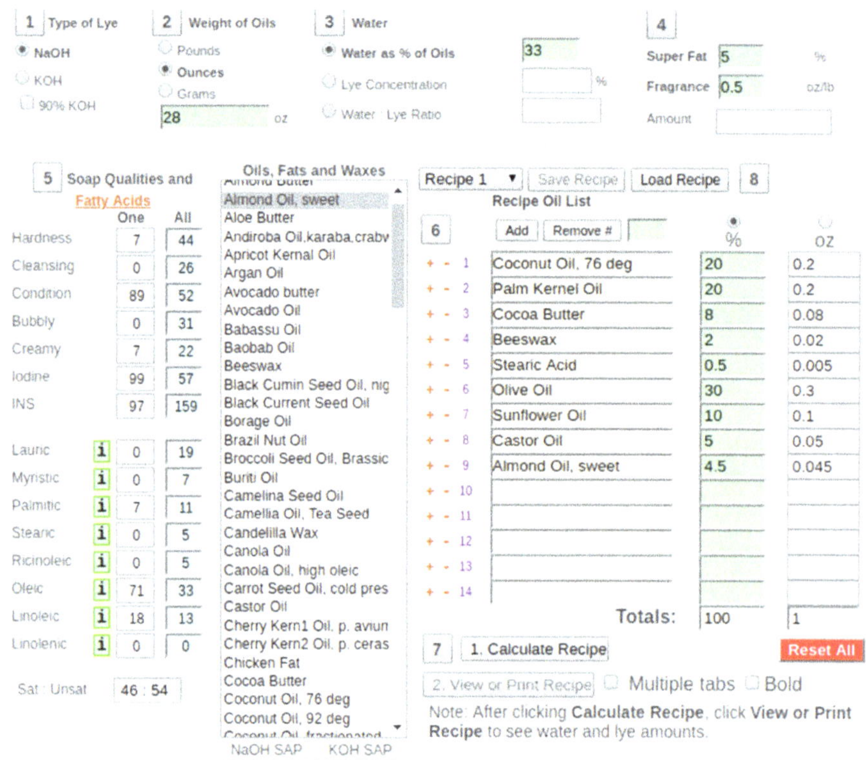

Don't forget to include the sodium lactate in the "Additives" section. Once you've added everything, hit "Calculate Recipe," and it will total the percentages up to 100. If the percentages don't make 100, it'll show you an error. Notice that this recipe will yield 28 ounces of soap, as you can see right now. This total will change once the lye and water are added. For reference, the basic rectangular soap molds usually hold almost 1200 grams or 42 ounces of soap.

Now, click "View or Print Recipe," and a separate tab will open. The page should look like this:

Total oil weight	28 oz	Sat : Unsat Ratio	46 : 54
Water as percent of oil weight	**33.00 %**	Iodine	57
Super Fat/Discount	5 %	INS	159
Lye Concentration	30.407 %	Fragrance Ratio	0.5
Water : Lye Ratio	2.2887:1	Fragrance Weight	0.88 oz

	Pounds	Ounces	Grams
Water	0.578	9.24	261.95
Lye - NaOH	0.252	4.04	114.45
Oils	1.750	28.00	793.79
Fragrance	0.055	0.88	24.81
Soap weight before CP cure or HP cook	2.635	42.15	1,194.99

#	√	Oil/Fat	%	Pounds	Ounces	Grams
1		Coconut Oil, 76 deg	20.00	0.350	5.60	158.76
2		Palm Kernel Oil	20.00	0.350	5.60	158.76
3		Cocoa Butter	8.00	0.140	2.24	63.50
4		Beeswax	2.00	0.035	0.56	15.88
5		Stearic Acid	0.50	0.009	0.14	3.97
6		Olive Oil	30.00	0.525	8.40	238.14
7		Sunflower Oil	10.00	0.175	2.80	79.38
8		Castor Oil	5.00	0.088	1.40	39.69
9		Almond Oil, sweet	4.50	0.079	1.26	35.72
		Totals	100.00	1.750	28.00	793.79

Soap Bar Quality	Range	Your Recipe		
Hardness	29 - 54	44	Lauric	19
Cleansing	12 - 22	26	Myristic	7
Conditioning	44 - 69	52	Palmitic	11
Bubbly	14 - 46	31	Stearic	5
Creamy	16 - 48	22	Ricinoleic	5
Iodine	41 - 70	57	Oleic	33
INS	136 - 165	159	Linoleic	13
			Linolenic	0

Additives	Notes

As you can see, "Soap weight before CP" will be 42.15 oz or 1195 grams. You can also add notes or additives in the section below. And that's about it! That's all there is to it! This will create a hard bar of soap that lasts quite a while.

But what about creaminess and lather? How do you create a recipe with these factors in mind?

Basic recipe with a little bit of everything (creaminess, lather, hardness, nourishment, etc.)

To make sure that you get the lather, conditioning, hardness, creaminess, and everything else in a basic recipe, I recommend 60% hard oils and 40% soft oils. Out of these, you can choose oils that are nourishing and luxurious while providing a creamy lather at the same time. If your budget allows you, you can also add almond and avocado oil.

So, we have:

60% hard oils (coconut oil, shea butter, and lard)

40% soft oils (olive oil, castor oil, avocado oil, and almond oil)

That would give you:

30% Coconut oil

10% Shea Butter

20% Lard

25% Olive oil

5% Castor oil

6% Avocado oil

4% Almond oil

1 teaspoon of Sodium lactate for every pound of oils

When you input everything on SoapCalc, you get:

SoapCalc ©	Recipe Name: Basic CP Soap			New	INCI Names	Print Recipe

Total oil weight	28 oz		Sat : Unsat Ratio		45 : 55
Water as percent of oil weight	**38.00 %**		Iodine		55
Super Fat/Discount	5 %		INS		158
Lye Concentration	27.243 %		Fragrance Ratio		0.5
Water : Lye Ratio	2.6707:1		Fragrance Weight		0.88 oz

	Pounds	**Ounces**	**Grams**
Water	0.665	10.64	301.64
Lye - NaOH	0.249	3.98	112.95
Oils	1.750	28.00	793.79
Fragrance	0.055	0.88	24.81
Soap weight before CP cure or HP cook	2.719	43.50	1,233.18

#	√	Oil/Fat	%	Pounds	Ounces	Grams
1		Coconut Oil, 76 deg	30.00	0.525	8.40	238.14
2		Shea Butter	10.00	0.175	2.80	79.38
3		Lard, Pig Tallow Manteca	20.00	0.350	5.60	158.76
4		Olive Oil	25.00	0.438	7.00	198.45
5		Castor Oil	5.00	0.088	1.40	39.69
6		Avocado Oil	6.00	0.105	1.68	47.63
7		Almond Oil, sweet	4.00	0.070	1.12	31.75
		Totals	100.00	1.750	28.00	793.79

Soap Bar Quality	Range	Your Recipe			
Hardness	29 - 54	42	Lauric	14	
Cleansing	12 - 22	20	Myristic	6	
Conditioning	44 - 69	52	Palmitic	14	
Bubbly	14 - 46	25	Stearic	8	
Creamy	16 - 48	27	Ricinoleic	5	
Iodine	41 - 70	55	Oleic	40	
INS	136 - 165	158	Linoleic	7	
			Linolenic	0	

Additives	Notes

Clicking on View or Print recipe will give you:

SoapCalc ®	Recipe Name:		New	INCI Names	Print Recipe

Total oil weight	42 oz	Sat : Unsat Ratio		45 : 55
Water as percent of oil weight	**38.00 %**	Iodine		55
Super Fat/Discount	5 %	INS		158
Lye Concentration	27.243 %	Fragrance Ratio		0.5
Water : Lye Ratio	2.6707:1	Fragrance Weight		1.31 oz

	Pounds	Ounces	Grams
Water	0.997	15.96	452.46
Lye - NaOH	0.374	5.98	169.42
Oils	2.625	42.00	1,190.68
Fragrance	0.082	1.31	37.22
Soap weight before CP cure or HP cook	4.078	65.25	1,849.78

#	√	Oil/Fat	%	Pounds	Ounces	Grams
1		Coconut Oil, 76 deg	30.00	0.787	12.60	357.20
2		Shea Butter	10.00	0.263	4.20	119.07
3		Lard, Pig Tallow Manteca	20.00	0.525	8.40	238.14
4		Olive Oil	25.00	0.656	10.50	297.67
5		Castor Oil	5.00	0.131	2.10	59.53
6		Avocado Oil	6.00	0.157	2.52	71.44
7		Almond Oil, sweet	4.00	0.105	1.68	47.63
		Totals	100.00	2.625	42.00	1,190.68

Soap Bar Quality	Range	Your Recipe		
Hardness	29 - 54	42	Lauric	14
Cleansing	12 - 22	20	Myristic	6
Conditioning	44 - 69	52	Palmitic	14
Bubbly	14 - 46	25	Stearic	8
Creamy	16 - 48	27	Ricinoleic	5
Iodine	41 - 70	55	Oleic	40
INS	136 - 165	158	Linoleic	7
			Linolenic	0

Additives	Notes

Of course, you still have to learn how to make the soap itself, but I hope this gives you a basic understanding of how to create your own recipes.

Chapter 7

How to Make Hot Process Soap

When I first began making soap, I started with Hot Process soap. Most people start with M&P, but I was drawn to HP because it allowed me to customize my oils exactly the way I wanted. Do you want to ensure you benefit from that shea butter? Or do you want to use that fragrance oil but are hesitant because it accelerates the process too much? Hot Process comes to your rescue!

The primary concept of the Hot Process is that you cook the soap to speed up saponification rather than letting the saponification occur naturally. It basically means that you're forcing saponification, and you can end up with a great bar of soap with moisturizing oils.

There are several ways of making HP soap. Many soapers use a crockpot, a method that I recommend but do not personally use. I make my HP soaps on the stove. Of course, you cannot place the soap directly on heat like you're cooking food. Instead, you can use a double boiler, an induction stove, or an oven.

Making HP soap is almost like cooking chicken. The only difference is that while chicken will still taste good even when you cook it on high heat, HP soap will surely burn. Thus, no matter the method of heat you use as you cook the soap, make sure you keep an eye on it. With experience, you'll probably change your method, but stick to basic rules until then. The trick to making amazing HP soap is to stop cooking it at the right time. Just like overcooked chicken, overcooked soap will not do you any good. HP soap turns crumbly when cooked too much, and crumbly soap is not fun at all.

As you go, you will learn that there's no specific method to cooking HP soap. You simply try different methods and stick to the method that makes you the most comfortable. As soon as you recognize the different stages of soap and act accordingly, you can start making more batches of soap than you've ever imagined.

Hot Process Soap Recipe

I wanted to make a really moisturizing soap that produced lots of lather. Of course, I needed it to be hard, too. So, I formulated this very simple recipe. As always, run it on SoapCalc if you want to tweak the recipe.

This recipe will yield 46.6 oz or 1321 grams of soap, which is just perfect for my mold.

Olive oil pomace – 510 grams

Coconut oil – 297.50 grams

Shea butter – 42.50 grams

Distilled water – 323 grams

Lye – 121.89 grams

Glycolic acid beads (optional)

Sodium lactate – 3 teaspoons

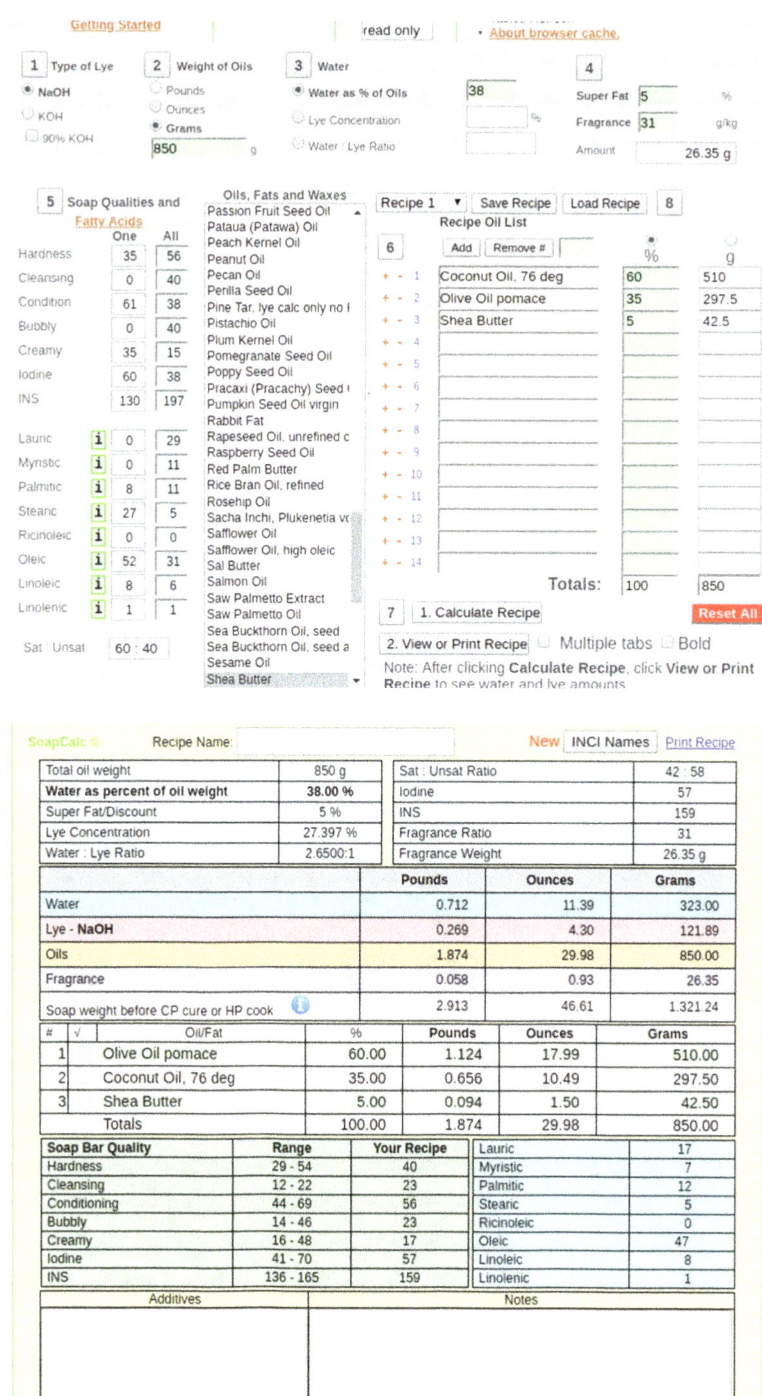

The lower reproduced printout:

Total oil weight	850 g	Sat : Unsat Ratio	42 : 58
Water as percent of oil weight	38.00 %	Iodine	57
Super Fat/Discount	5 %	INS	159
Lye Concentration	27.397 %	Fragrance Ratio	31
Water : Lye Ratio	2.6500:1	Fragrance Weight	26.35 g

	Pounds	Ounces	Grams
Water	0.712	11.39	323.00
Lye - NaOH	0.269	4.30	121.89
Oils	1.874	29.98	850.00
Fragrance	0.058	0.93	26.35
Soap weight before CP cure or HP cook	2.913	46.61	1.321.24

#	√	Oil/Fat	%	Pounds	Ounces	Grams
1		Olive Oil pomace	60.00	1.124	17.99	510.00
2		Coconut Oil, 76 deg	35.00	0.656	10.49	297.50
3		Shea Butter	5.00	0.094	1.50	42.50
		Totals	100.00	1.874	29.98	850.00

Soap Bar Quality	Range	Your Recipe		
Hardness	29 - 54	40	Lauric	17
Cleansing	12 - 22	23	Myristic	7
Conditioning	44 - 69	56	Palmitic	12
Bubbly	14 - 46	23	Stearic	5
Creamy	16 - 48	17	Ricinoleic	0
Iodine	41 - 70	57	Oleic	47
INS	136 - 165	159	Linoleic	8
			Linolenic	1

Additives	Notes

I will use the shea butter as the super fat, so it gently moisturizes the skin. You can use any other oil you want, but since the SAP values will be different, be sure to run through it on SoapCalc first. The best part of making HP soap is that you don't need to plan too extensively while making the soap. Even if there are a few spills, you can clean it immediately because it has been saponified in the cooking process.

So, prepare your work area and gather your tools, just like you would for CP soap. If you're using a crockpot, go ahead and set it on your workspace. You should ensure that all of your ingredients ultimately end up in the crockpot to be cooked, so keep this in mind as you add your ingredients together. If you love using steel utensils like me, follow the steps mentioned below. Of course, *don't* forget to wear gloves and goggles because you're still going to be dealing with lye.

1) Measure and heat your oils

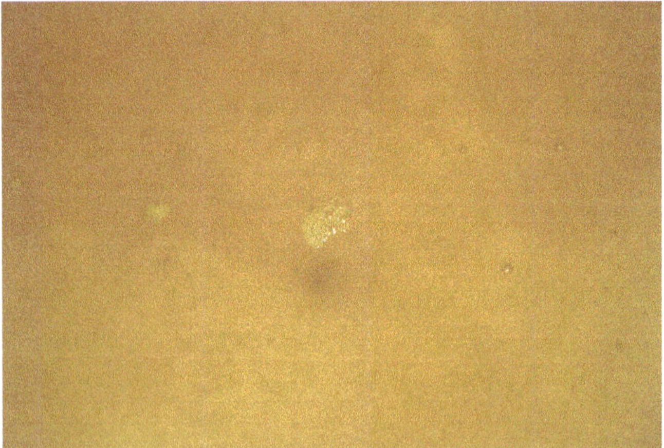

Measure the coconut oil and olive oil. You can add the shea butter later when the soap has finished cooking. Place the container in the microwave and heat it in 30-second bursts, or follow your preferred, non-direct heating method.

2) Measure the water amount

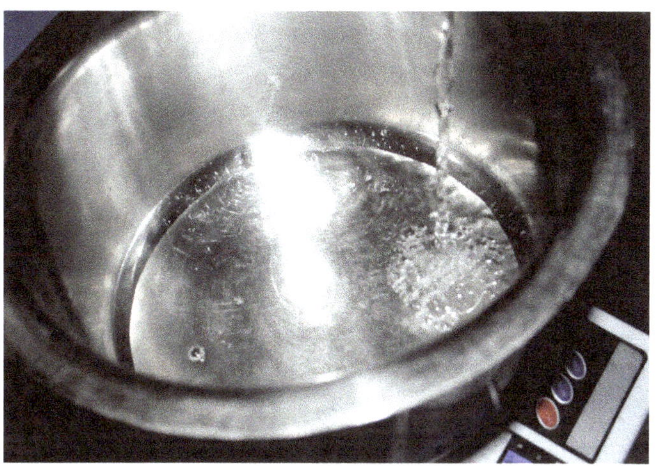

Once again, I recommend that you use distilled water only. Measure it and set it aside.

3) Measure the lye

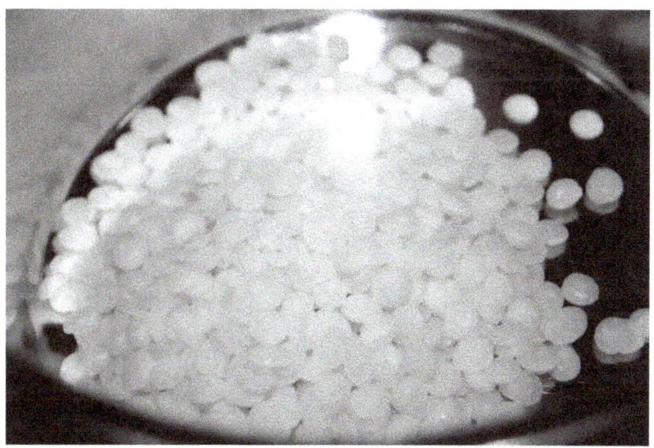

As always, do this after measuring oils and water.

4) Make lye water solution

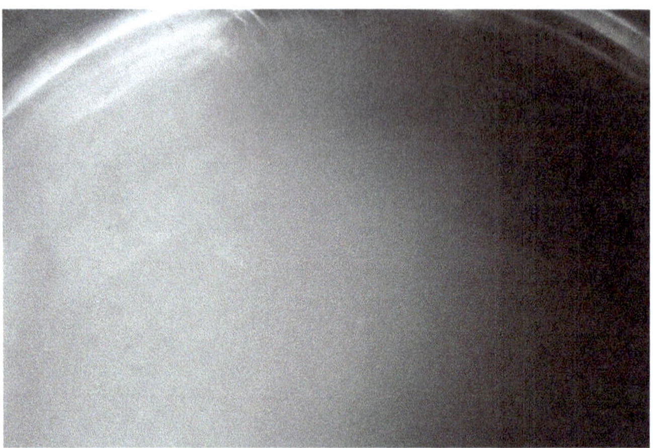

Using a steel container, slowly pour the lye into the water. Remember never to pour water into the lye. Mix the solution until all the lye dissolves.

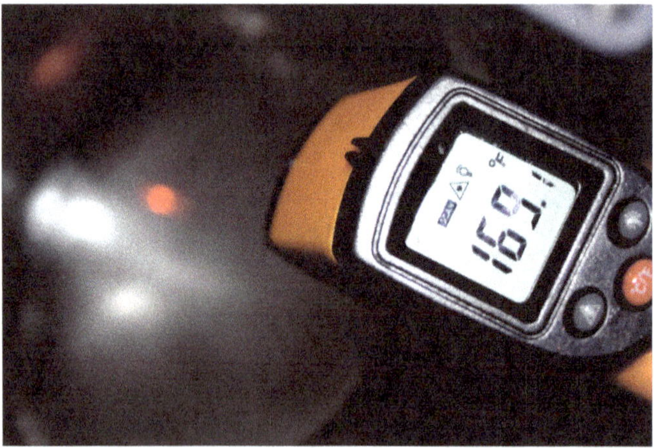

Set it aside carefully and wait for it to cool down to at least 120 to 130°F and turn clear. Once it turns clear, add sodium lactate.

5) Measure the remaining ingredients

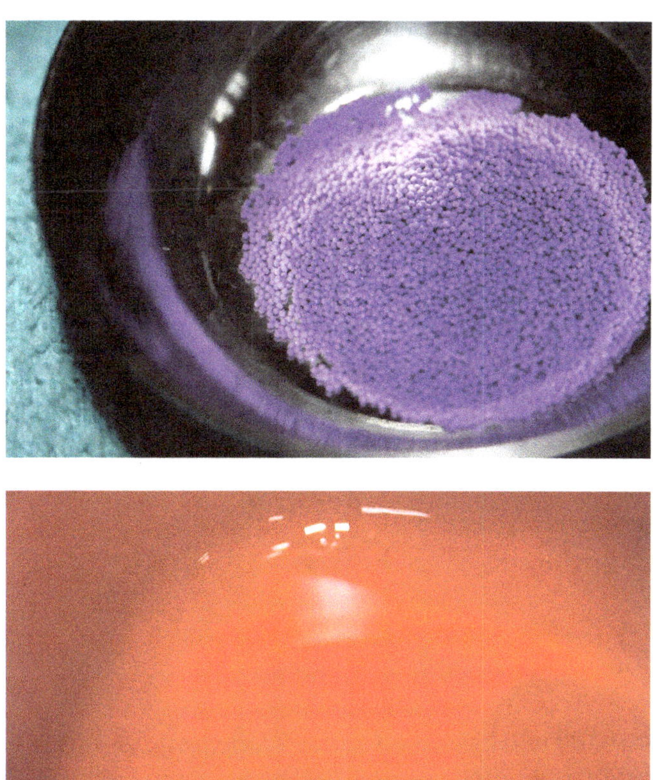

While the lye solution is cooling, measure the other ingredients, such as fragrance oils and other additives. I used glycolic acid beads in this recipe, so I measured about 1 tablespoon. Glycolic acid beads, although optional, serve as a scrub and also make the soap prettier! There's no exact amount when it comes to additives like beads, oats, or dried flowers. Therefore, you can use as much as you think is necessary.

6) Check the temperatures

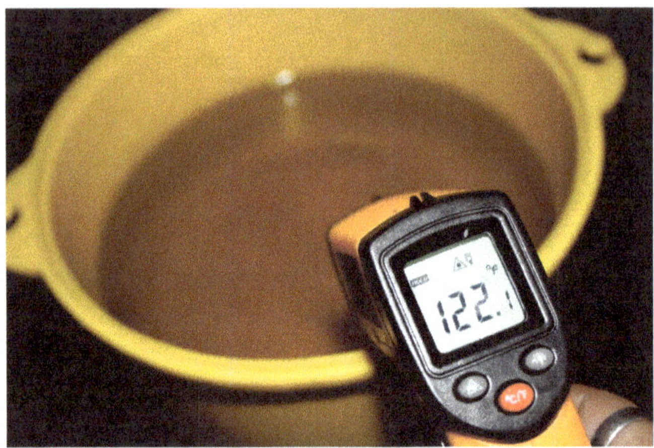

Check the temperatures of both the oils and lye again. Like CP soap, they need to be within about 10 degrees of each other, so anything from 110 to 130 degrees is fine. Of course, you can reheat as needed.

7) Combine oils and lye water

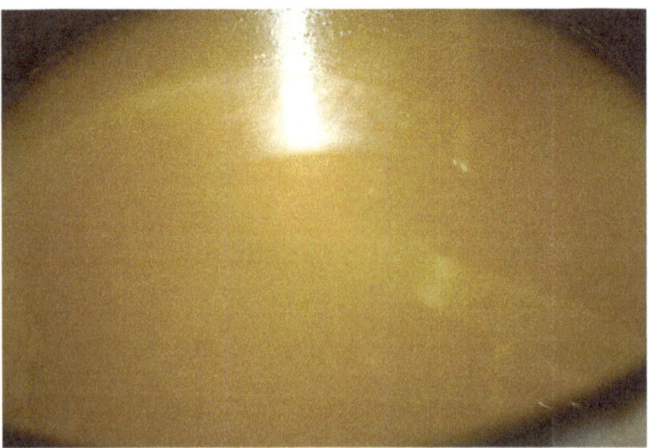

Once you're satisfied with the temperatures, combine the oils and lye solution. Start by mixing the mixture with a spatula.

After a few minutes of mixing, switch to the immersion blender. Make sure that you use the blender only at the bottom of the container, or it'll spill all over! With CP soap, you'll want to keep an eye on the trace, but with HP soap, you don't have to bother.

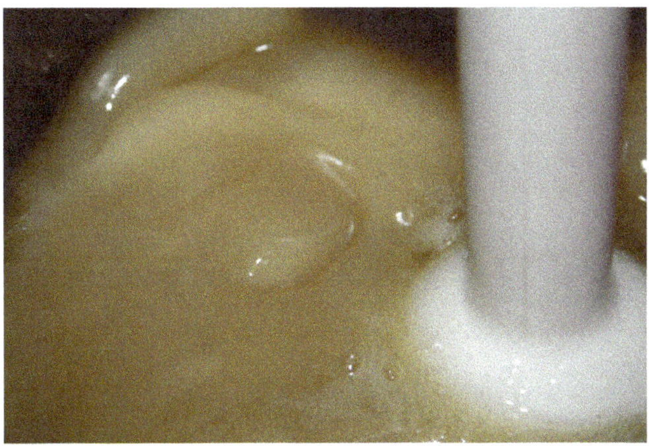

Use the blender to emulsify the mixture completely, and you'll notice it turns milky. Tap the blender up and down periodically to get rid of any air bubbles. Once it has thickened considerably, you can stop using the blender.

I hope these pictures speak for themselves.

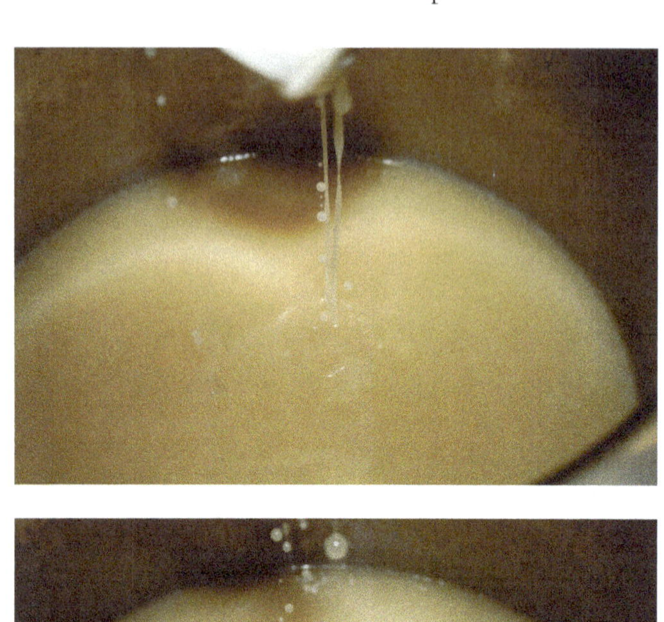

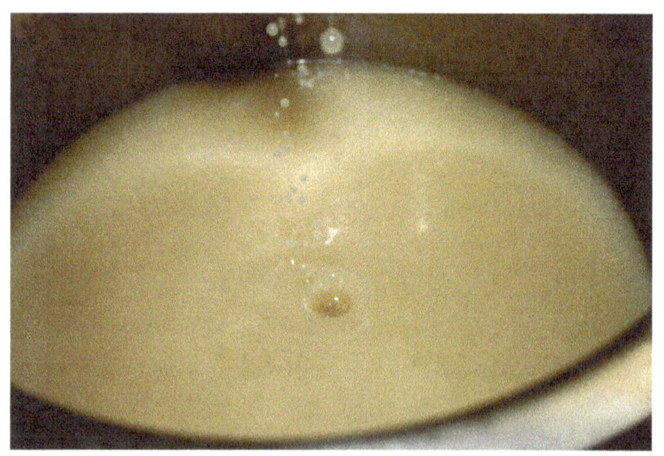

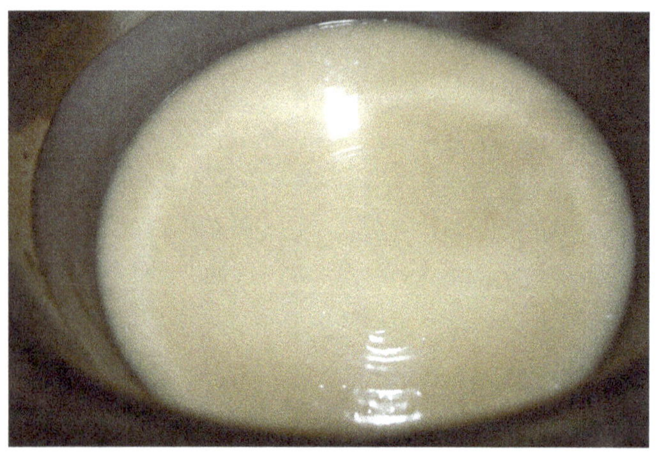

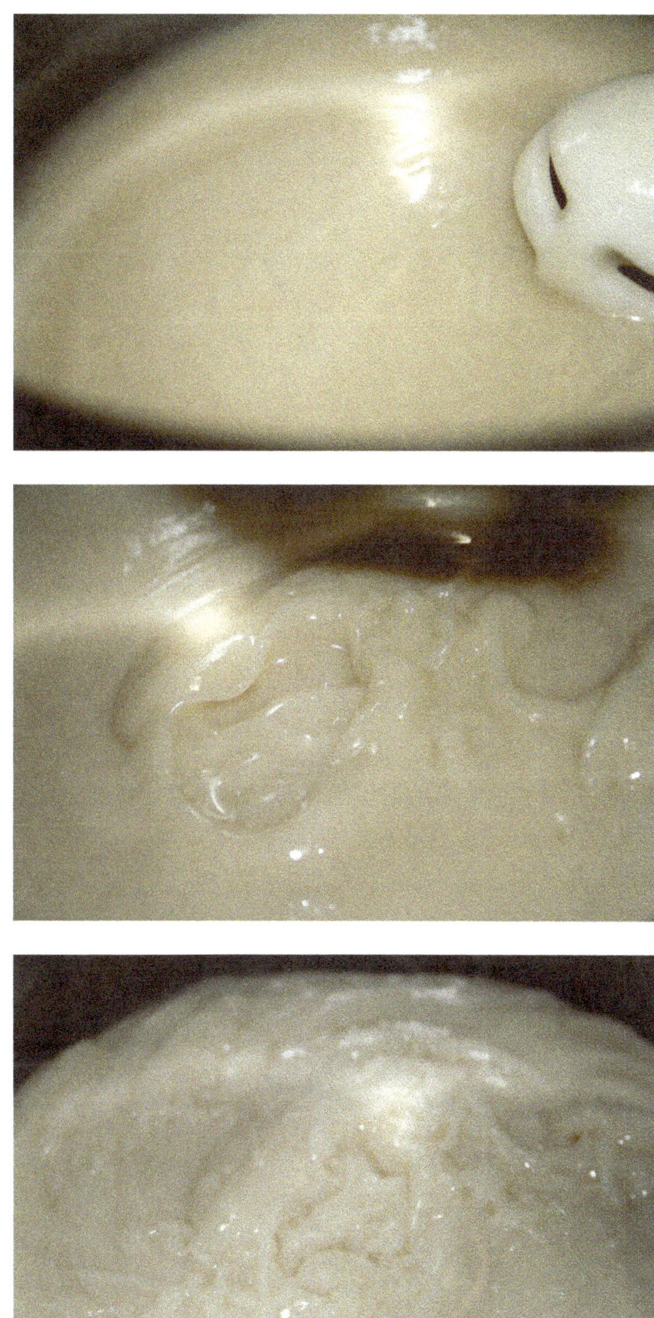

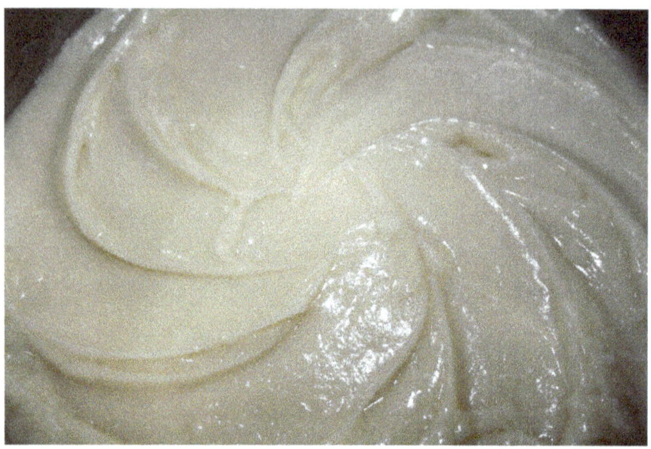

8) Cook the soap

If you've been using a crockpot, this is, of course, where you have been mixing everything from the start, and you will now cover it with a lid to begin cooking the soap. If you've been using steel containers as I do, make sure to set up a double boiler, as direct heat on your soap will cause problems. A pot filled with water placed below the steel container will work well for this purpose.

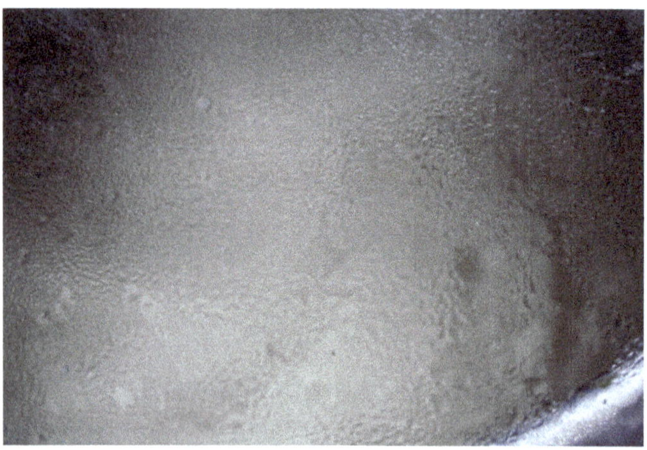

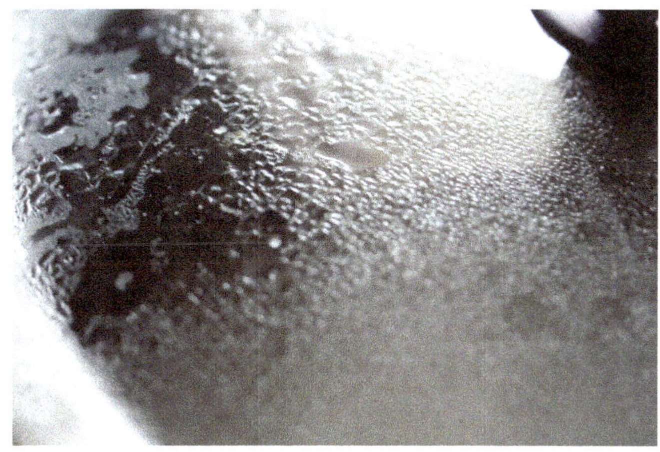

I have used an induction stove to cook my soap. You can't see the soap with all the steam, but it's there! You can choose to heat it in any way you want as long as there's no direct heat. If you introduce direct heat, you'll burn your soap pretty quickly! Burnt soap smells nasty, so you really don't want to experience that!

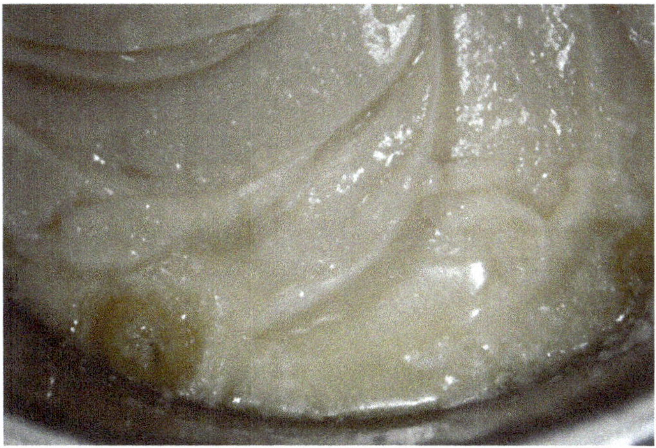

Once the soap starts cooking, you want to pay close attention, especially if you're a beginner. The soap goes through several stages. If it looks like it's going to surge out of the pot, quickly stir it back in using a spatula. Recipes with a lot of sugar tend to volcano out of the pot, and it can occur, especially when the soap's too hot. This is why you need to keep a close eye on the soap at all times.

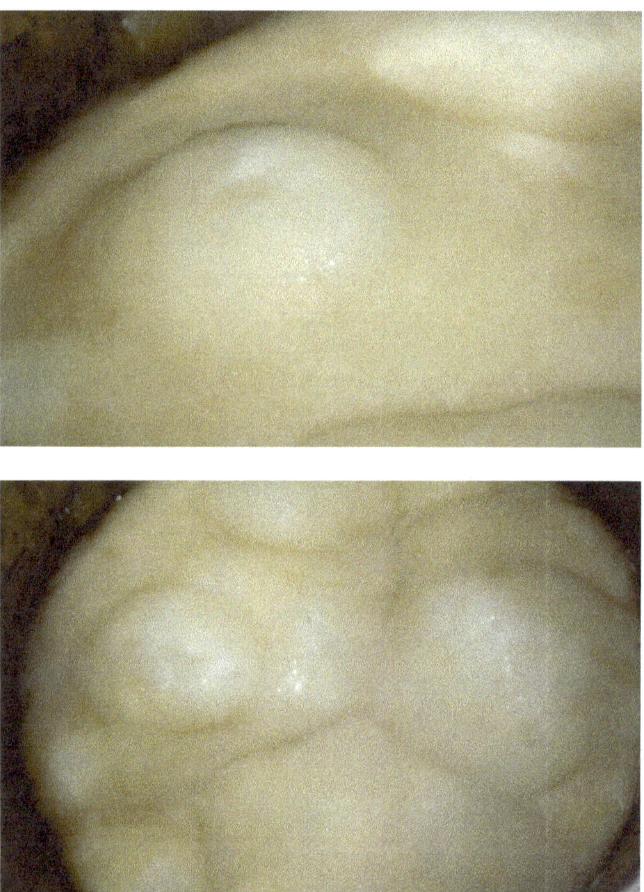

The soap changes from one stage to another as it cooks. If you have a big batch, it takes more time, but smaller batches can be cooked in about thirty minutes to an hour. The first stage is the Pudding Stage where the soap looks like – you guessed it – pudding. Stir everything once again, and it enters the second stage, known as the Applesauce Stage. Unsurprisingly, this stage resembles applesauce.

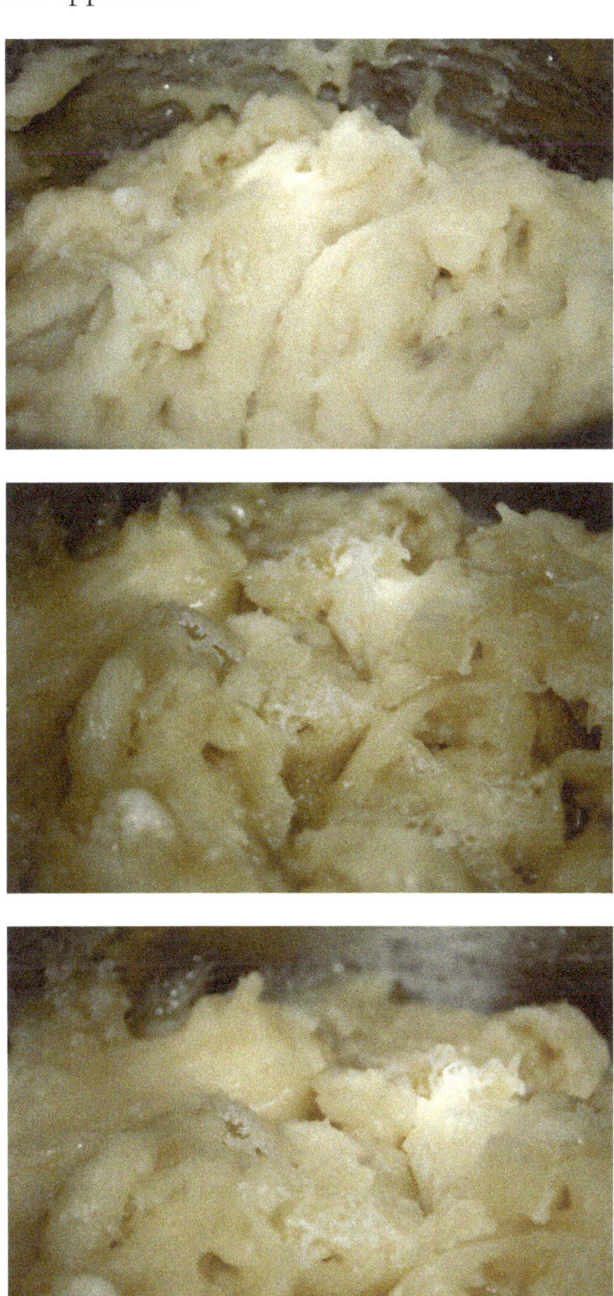

As the soap gets cooked, it enters the Vaseline Stage, in which it appears almost translucent, like petroleum jelly. The edges of the soap will gel faster because that's the hottest part of the soap. Scrap the sides of the container back to the center of the pot and let it cook a while more. Once the soap reaches the Vaseline stage and appears like wax, it's time to turn off the heat.

"But how do I know if the soap is completely cooked without any lye residue?" you ask. Well, there are several ways to find out. One is the zap test, in which you place a small amount of soap on your tongue. Others use pH strips or pH meters, but these can be inaccurate. If you're a beginner, the best way to test is to use Phenolphthalein drops.

If you want to do the zap test, simply wet your fingertip, take a small amount of soap, and place it on your tongue. If you feel something like a static shock, it's lye-heavy and needs to be cooked more. If you just find the taste bitter or metallic with no zap, then the soap is done.

Be careful with this method because the soap can burn your tongue if there's a lot of lye still remaining. I use Phenolphthalein drops because I don't like to torture myself, but if you don't have it, you can also do the zap test after the soap has rested for a day or two.

To test with the Phenolphthalein drops, take a small amount of soap and place it on a tissue paper like this:

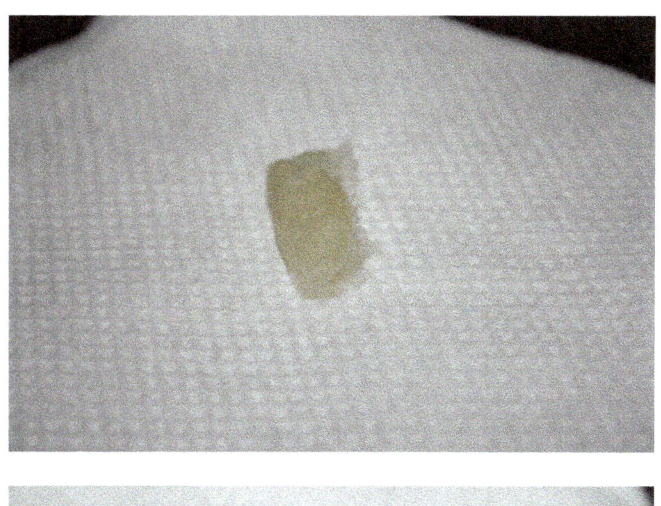

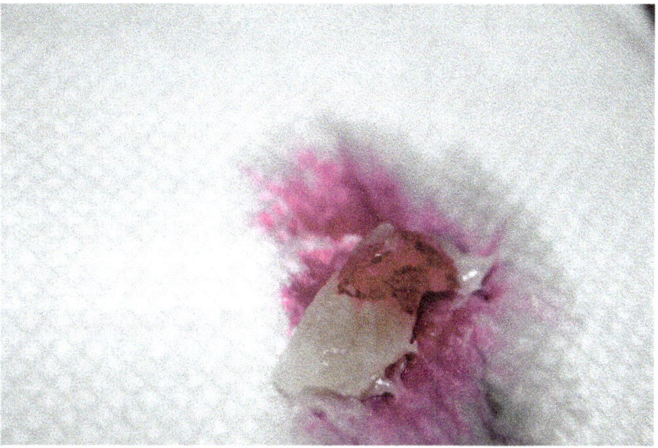

Next, pour a drop or two of the Phenolphthalein solution. If the soap turns purple, it's lye-heavy, and you should let it cook longer before pouring it into a mold. The picture above definitely shows that there's a lot of lye remaining in the soap!

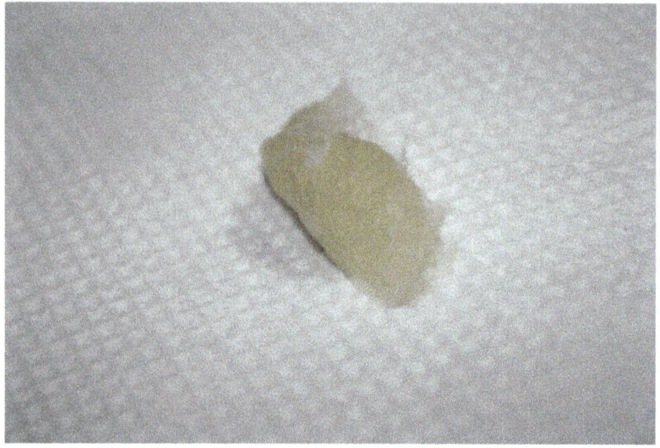

If there's no lye left in the soap, there's no color at all. You may see a very slight purple tint at times, but it will disappear if the soap is cooked more. Now, there's no lye remaining, and the soap is ready to be poured into the mold.

9) Add other additives

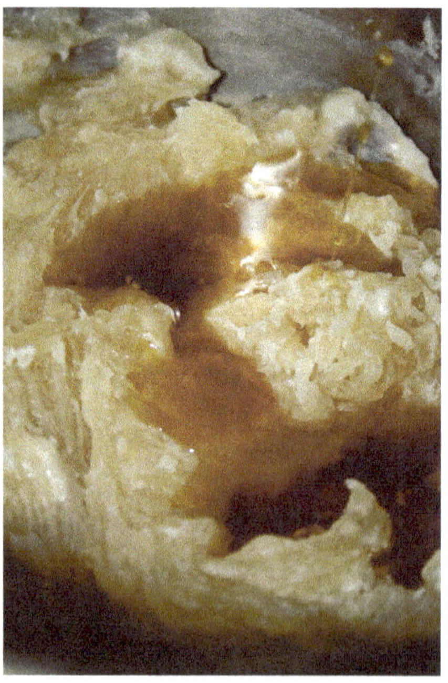

Once the soap is cooled a little (but not very much, or you won't be able to mold it), you can add additives like fragrance oil and colors. This is also where you measure your super fat and add it. I will add my shea butter and glycolic beads at this point.

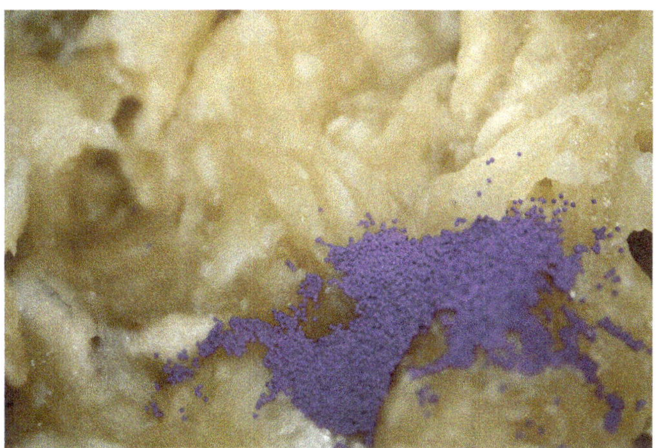

If you add the fragrance oil when the soap is too hot, it will fade due to the heat. I recommend waiting until the soap has cooled down to at least 160 to 170 degrees to add fragrance.

10) Mold the soap

Finally, it's time to mold the soap. Unlike CP soap, you only have to plop the soap into the mold. Remember to tap the mold periodically, or you'll end up with ugly air bubbles and holes in the soap!

To make my soap a little more interesting, I scooped only half the batter into the mold at first. I am adding yellow mica dissolved in some isopropyl alcohol to the remaining batter. (You can also mix it with shea butter if you don't want to use alcohol). I will also sprinkle some activated charcoal to create a thin line between both batters. Finally, it's time to mold the soap.

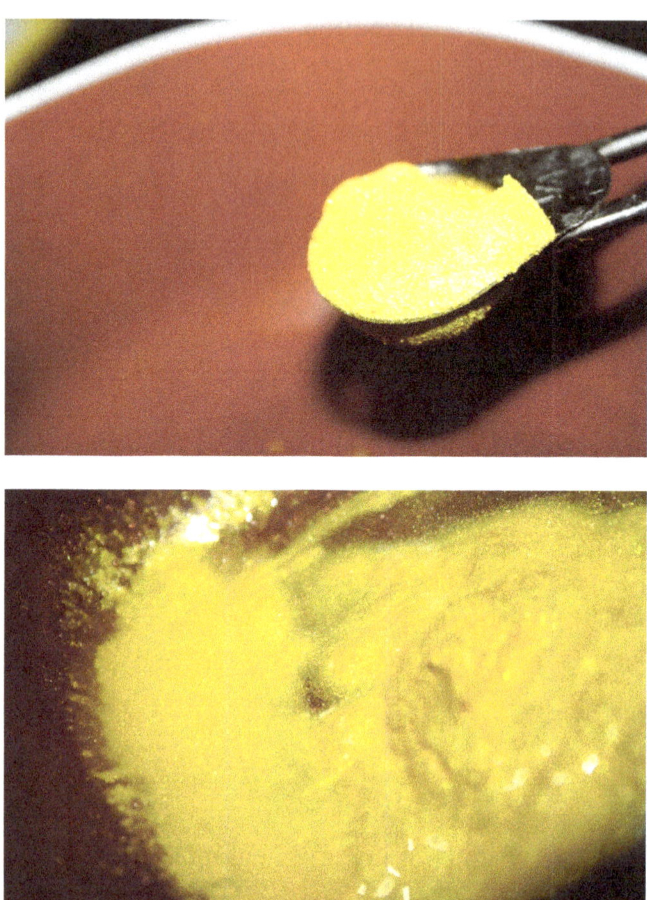

If you're keen to use anything for aesthetic purposes, like glitter or dry flowers, add them as soon as you've finished plopping the batter into the mold. Use a spatula to even out the sides, and then add your decorative elements. Remember to use them while the soap is still warm so it sticks better. Set the mold aside in a warm area, and you're done!

11) Cut the soap

Most HP recipes yield soaps that can be cut within 24-48 hours. Some can be cut even faster if only hard oils are used. I generally wait for at least 24 hours so that the soap isn't mushy. A simple cheese cutter or knife will help you cut slices perfectly.

12) Cure the soap

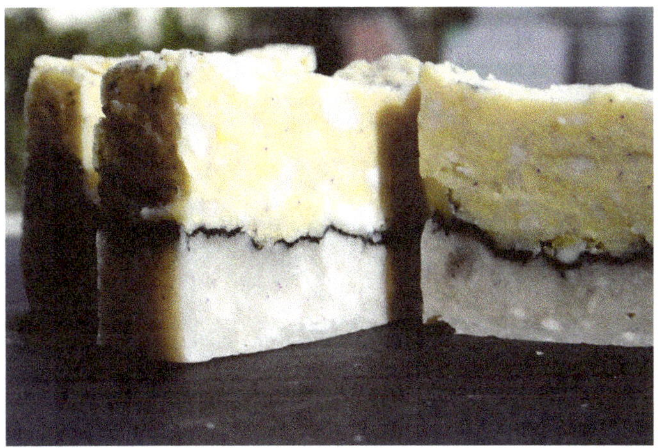

HP soaps don't need to be cured for weeks like CP soap. Many soapers use the soaps immediately because the saponification process is complete. However, it's best to let it cure for at least 1-2 weeks to ensure that it's rock-hard.

Chapter 8

How to Make Melt and Pour Soap

Melt and Pour soaps are the easiest to make. Even kids can make them if you supervise them! Since you don't have to worry about lye at all, it's easier to introduce kids to soap-making with this method. And you can use it as soon as it's unmolded! What's not to like? Many soapers start with Melt and Pour and then shift to Cold Process or Hot Process once they gain confidence. You can do the same.

So, what do you need to make M&P soap? You need the base, of course. I have seen people trying to melt their regular commercial soaps to remake soaps, but that's not going to work. Just buy a soap base or make one from scratch like me!

I wasn't happy with the soap bases I purchased. So, like everything else, I made my own. However, you don't have to because it's a little more complicated than just regular soap. If you're a beginner, just buy some of those M&P soap bases that are available in varieties, including goat milk, honey, activated charcoal, transparent base, and more.

You start with a base just like this.

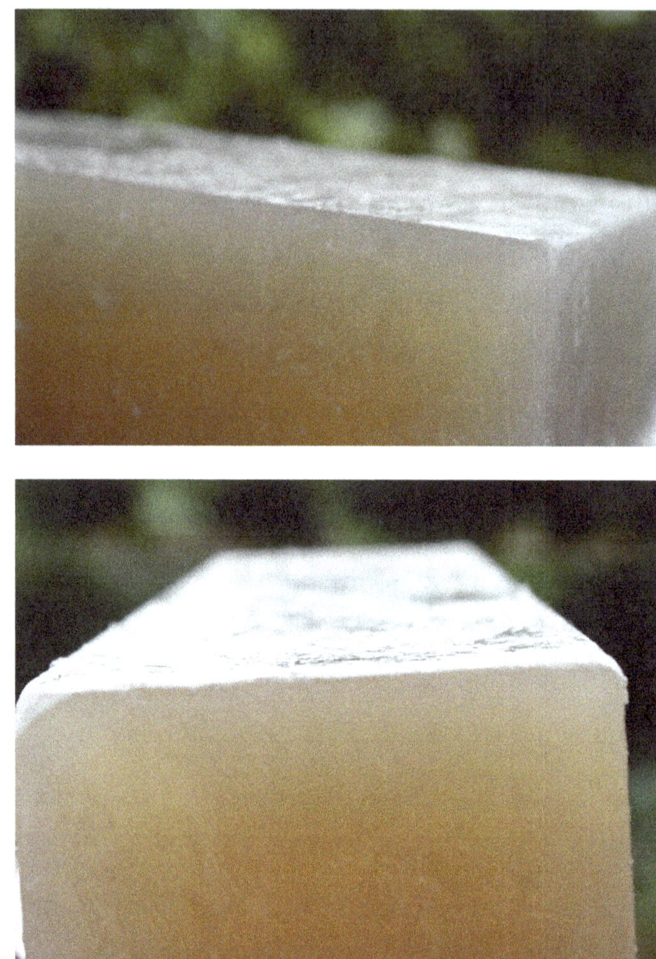

It's a clear base without any extra additives. The color is slightly tinted due to the colors of the oils used. Clear bases allow you to play with other ingredients and customize your soap. You can purchase M&P bases in any craft store. While some of them smell a tad like alcohol, you can hunt for bases that allow you to work with them longer and don't smell too bad.

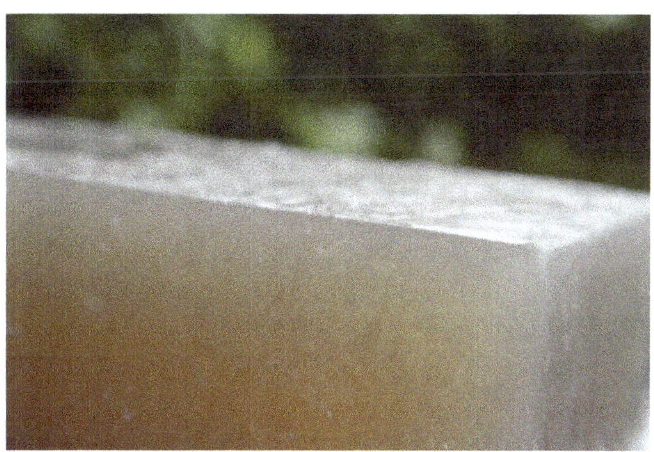

I chose to make soap that resembled a beach with waves. Here's the recipe:

Clear melt and pour soap base – 1000 grams

Bright blue mica – 1 tsp

Green mica – 1 tsp

Titanium dioxide – 1 tsp

Gold mica – 1 tsp

Walnut kernel powder – 1 tsp

Bergamot essential oil – 20 ml

To start off, cut the base into several cubes so that it melts faster. Some commercial bases harden and form a film as soon as they are heated. While it doesn't affect the outcome of the recipe, it means that you have to work faster.

Don't heat the soap too much, or you risk burning it. Microwave the cubes in quick 30-second bursts, or you'll have a lot of fumes forming inside the microwave. Stir the cubes after every 30-second interval since they tend to melt faster. There should be no lumps in the container before you start mixing colors.

Here are the steps to make the soap.

1) Cut 250 grams of soap base and melt it in the microwave. Set aside the remaining soap base – we'll need it later.

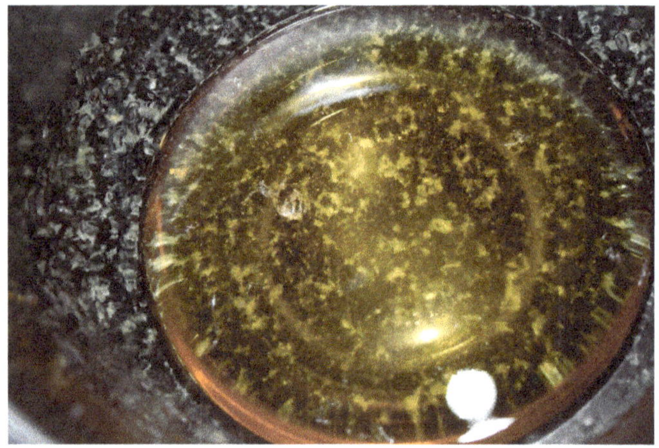

You can also melt the base with a double boiler, but a microwave works just fine. If the soap is too hot, wait until it cools down to at least 120°F or 49°C so that the walnut kernel powder is evenly dispersed. Also, the fragrance oil will fade away quickly if you work with a super hot base.

Why am I using walnut kernel powder specifically? Well, it resembles fine sand! My idea was to start with a brown or golden base that resembled sand.

2) Add colorants

Here, I have used gold mica. I had run out of brown colors, but you can use anything you choose.

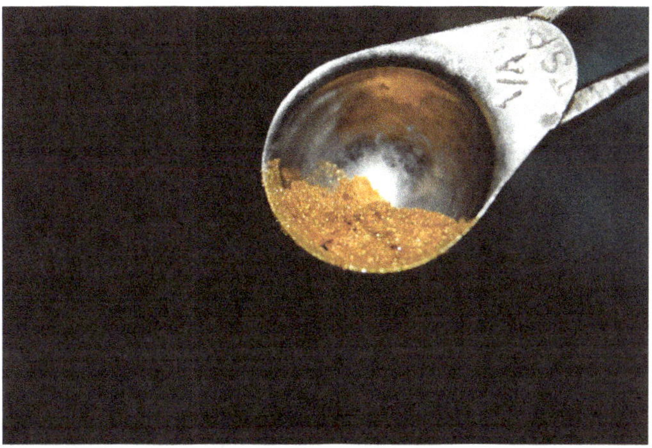

Mix the colors well. There should be no clumps.

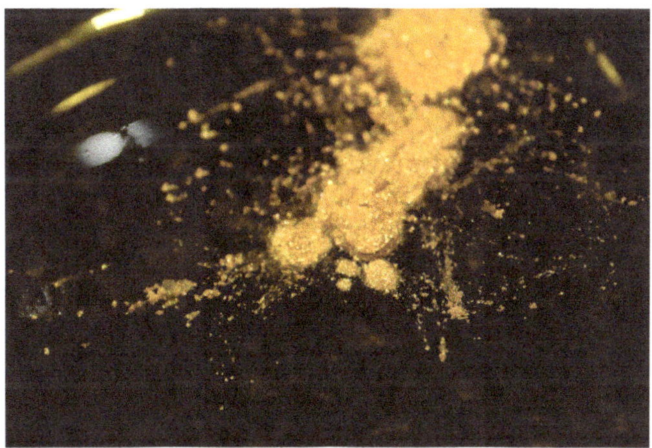

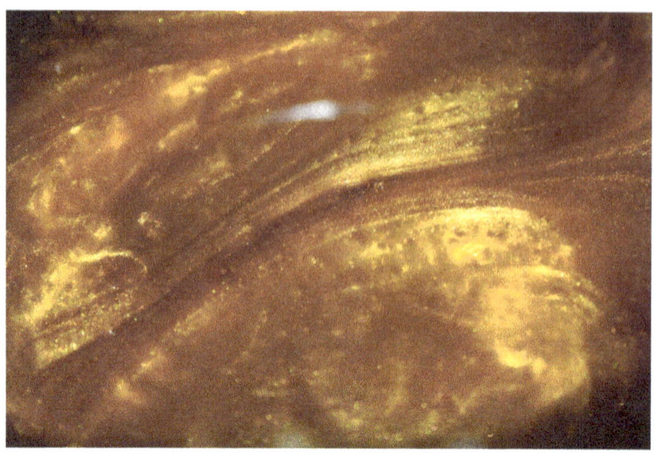

3) Add fragrance

Add about 5ml of your chosen fragrance oil. I have used Bergamot essential oil, and it smells divine. Mix well.

4) Add the additives

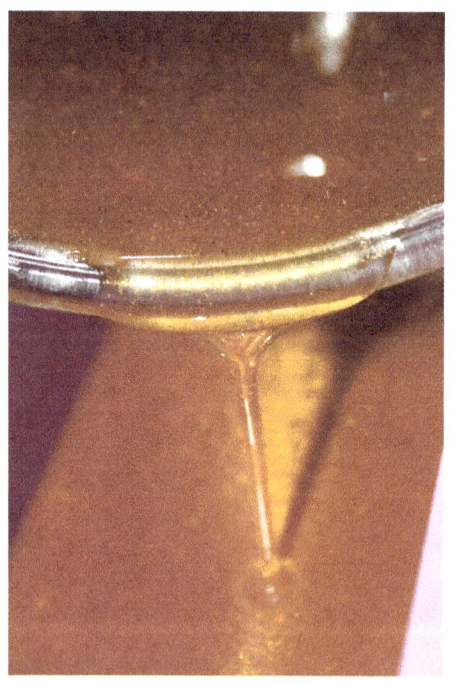

Add the walnut kernel powder. Stir again. Pour it into the mold. Wait until the soap sets in the mold. Don't wait too long, though! If the soap is too cold, the next layer will not stick to it, and you'll end up trying to stick them together unsuccessfully. Once the soap sets and is still warm, grab a spoon and make indents on it to make the sand look natural. If the soap oozes out while making indents, that's okay!

5) Cut another 250 grams of the base

Melt it in the microwave. Add blue mica and stir vigorously. Remember, there should be no clumps. Add 5ml essential oil. Pour the soap on top of the gold soap.

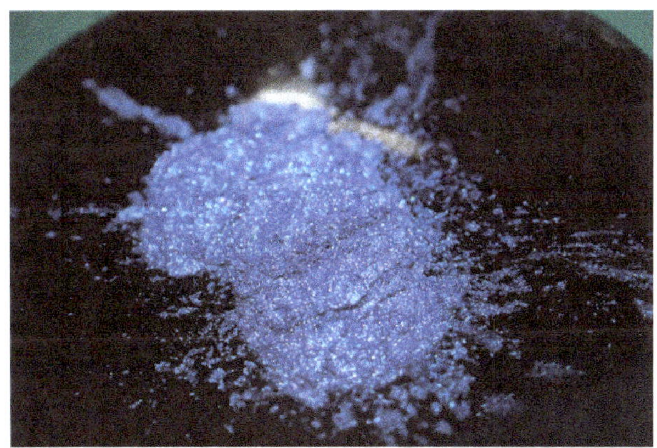

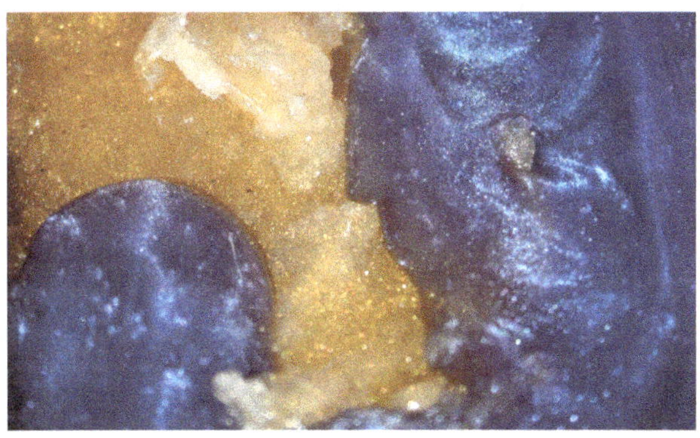

6) Cut the remaining 500 grams

Cut the remaining 500 grams and divide them into 2 different containers. Add green in one container while adding titanium dioxide in the other and stir well. Add 10 ml of essential oil. Pour the layers to make them look like waves.

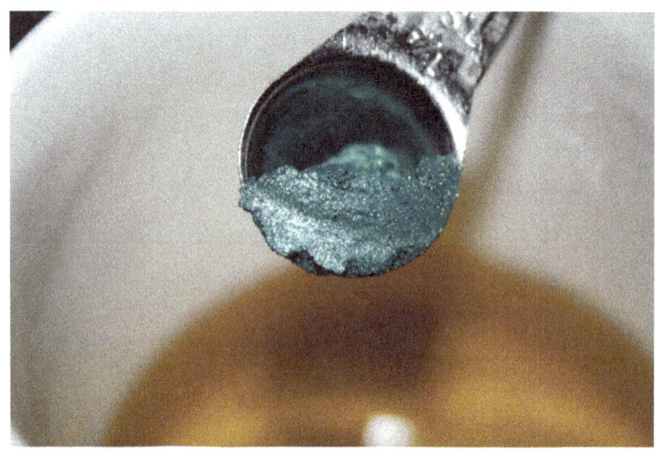

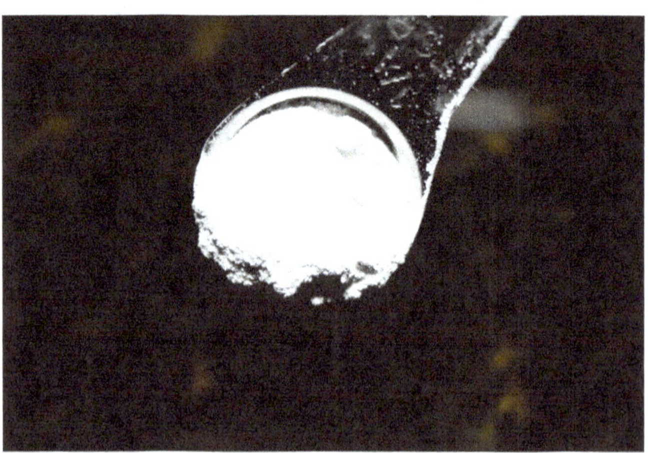

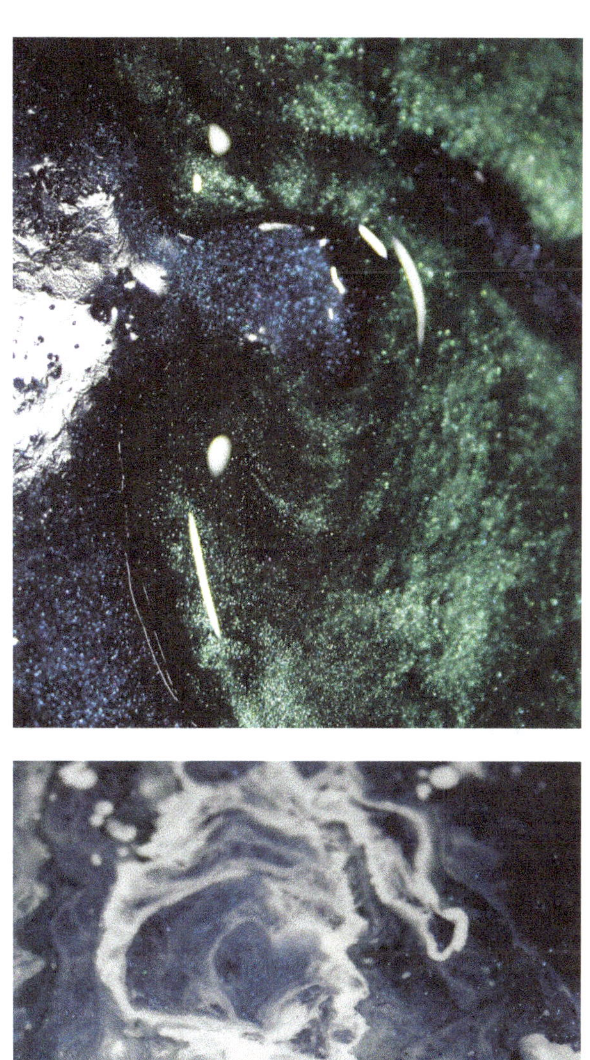

And that's it! Wait until it sets. You can cut the soap in about 6-7 hours, but they harden best if left alone for at least 24 hours. You now have your soap that (hopefully!) resembles waves on the beach.

7) Allow the soap to set

You don't have to wait too long for M&P to set. But, once it does set, cut into bars immediately and wrap them with shrink wrap. This is because M&P tends to sweat due to the high content of glycerin. And you have your own beautiful M&P soaps that can be used right away!

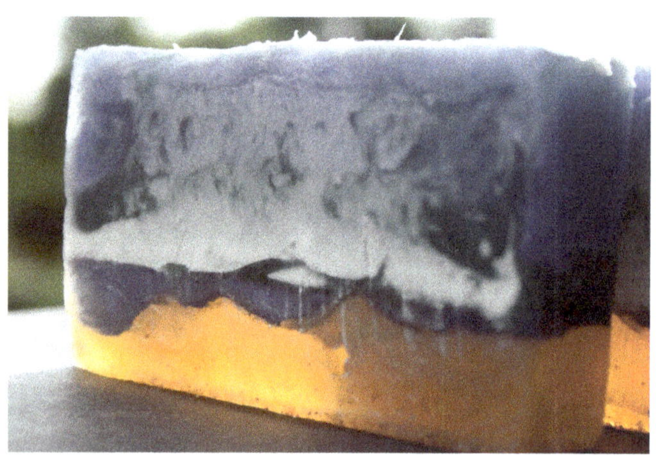

Chapter 9

Soap-making Issues

We are now going to talk about every soaper's nightmare. Some soapers have the ability to make every kind of soap – HP, CP, CPOP, M&P, soap embeds, etc. - you name it, and they can do it. However, mastering this process takes a lot of experience. And that experience doesn't come overnight. Behind all those wonderful techniques, you see, there are years of toil.

Not to mention the possibility that you can fail even if you've mastered the art of soap-making. Yes, even experienced soapers can still make a bad batch of soap. There may be times when nothing works, and the soap simply refuses to behave. You can tear your hair apart all you want and still miserably fail at it. It happens to the best of the best. But the best soapers learn from their mistakes and get better every day.

So, my dear reader – don't panic if your soap is messed up. At worst, you could simply start all over again. Or you can prepare yourself for what you can do if something goes wrong. And trust me, a lot can go wrong. This is not to scare you but to make you aware of the issues you could face.

A lot of the problems you face with the soap batter usually have something to do with the fragrance oil. I have already mentioned this while talking about fragrance oils. If you encounter an issue with your fragrance oil, it's likely that you're either using an oil that's past its expiry date or the synthetic material used to make the oil accelerates the problem.

You can also face issues if your lye is old. For instance, lye generally heats up to almost 170-200°F and is even hotter in some cases. If you notice that your lye doesn't get hot enough as soon as it's mixed with the water, it's probably old. Also, lye water should clear up within 10-15 minutes. If your lye solution stays cloudy for too long, there's a problem with the lye. In such cases, you can simply use the old lye as a drain cleaner and purchase a new batch!

Old oils can even make the soap smell rancid, and it's not something you want for yourself or for the recipients of your soaps.

This is why it is important to remember to use ingredients that are fairly new.

Coming back to the fragrance oils, here are a few potential problems you'll face in your soaping journey:

1) **Ricing** – Ricing is mainly caused by excessive use of fragrance oils. It can also occur due to a particular compound in the fragrance oil itself. Since the synthetic chemicals present in the fragrance oil binds with the harder compounds of the oils in the recipe, they form clumps. At first glance, it looks like rice pudding.

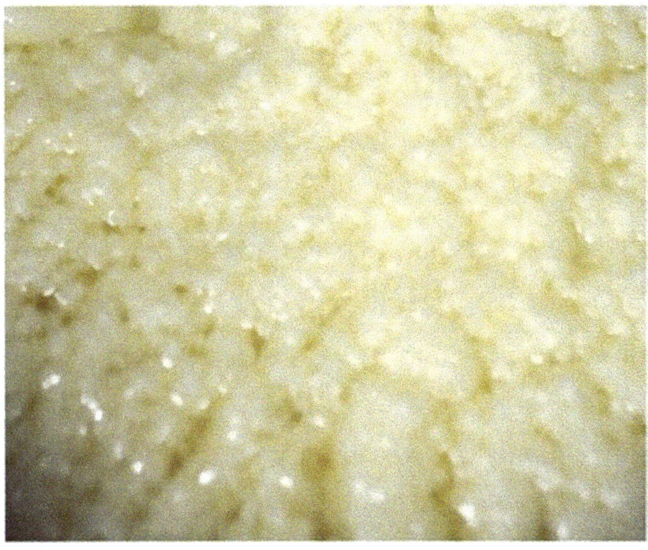

Soap ricing

It can make you panic since it gets worse as the blender tries its best to mix everything. But there's no need to panic. Just make a note of the fragrance oil used and the amount you used. If you just love the fragrance, you can test it in small batches with a smaller amount of fragrance. If the issue reappears again, you should probably only use that particular fragrance oil while making HP or M&P soaps. It's just not compatible with CP soaps.

But now, you've already mixed the oils, lye, and fragrance oils for your soap. You see the pudding-like mixture has riced and is looking as ugly as possible. Do you throw the batter away? No! There's a solution for everything!

The solution: Use the blender to mix up the oils as best as you can. Yes, it will get thicker. At this point, plop the batter onto the mold. If it's not possible, try to shift the batter to your crockpot and cook the batter. Just continue as you would with HP soap, and you should be able to salvage the batch. This way, you'll still save the soap.

If the batter is so thick that it can't be hot processed either, mold the soap and wait a few days to let the saponification process complete as usual. At worst, it can be used as laundry soap if the lye is still active. If not, you can still use it in the shower! The only issue is that it might appear a bit weird, but soapers really don't like to waste anything!

2) **Separation** – As the name suggests, separation is a problem that occurs when the fragrance oils cannot bind with the other oils. Due to this incompatibility, the oils just separate, and the fragrance oil pools at the top. The separation is so clearly visible that the soap looks like it's going to fall apart any minute!

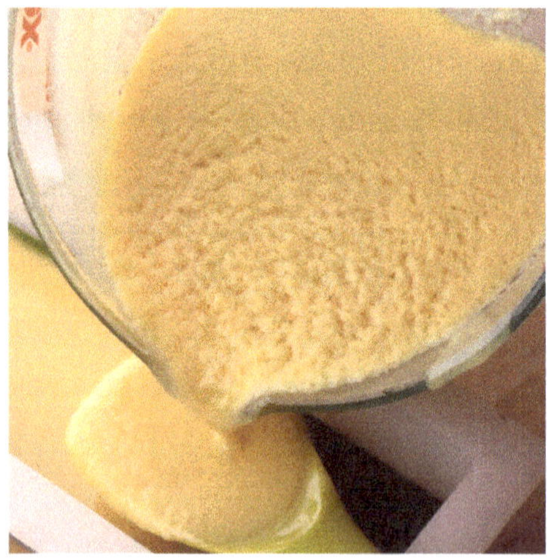

Soap Separation

3) **Seizing** – This is one of the most common problems you will face, especially if you're new to soap-making. Seizing is the term referred to the soap batter becoming unusually thick very fast. If the seize is minor, the batter becomes hard, but you'll still have time to mix it as fast as you can and fill it into your mold. But if the size is major, the batter becomes thick – like cement – right in front of your eyes in a matter of seconds.

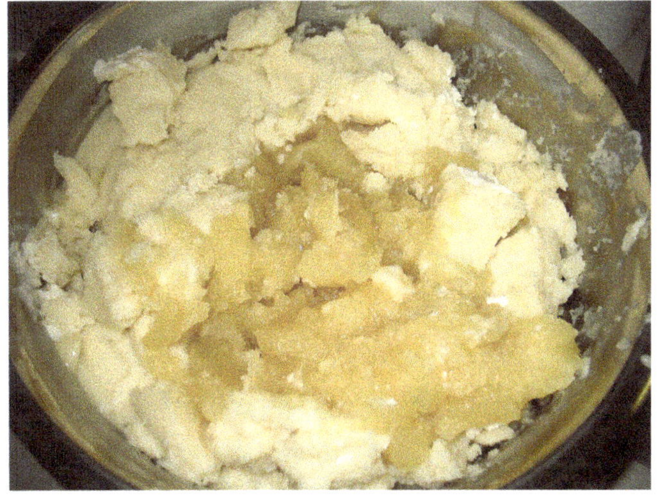

Soap Seizing

It usually occurs when the saponification between the lye and oils goes too fast. Floral fragrances are notorious for causing seizing. The best way to avoid seizing is to check the manufacturer's information before purchasing the fragrance oil. Usually, manufacturers will tell you whether the oil is prone to accelerate.

The Solution: If you already have a fragrance oil that can accelerate and cause seizing, make sure you keep the lye and oils at low temperatures to slow down the saponification. Also, don't try to reduce the water. In fact, stick to the measurements as shown in SoapCalc. You can also dilute the fragrance oils with some of the warm oils before adding the lye. Then, you add the oil + fragrance oil mixture at the very last minute, mix it, and pour it onto the mold.

Remember that you won't face this problem with M&P and HP soaps. You can always change plans at the last minute and stick to either of the two methods to avoid problems.

4) **Soap Volcano** – Sometimes, the soap batter heats to such an extent that it overflows out of the container that you are using. It's just lye-heavy, frothy soap oozing everywhere, and you have to act quickly. This problem can also be caused by fragrance oils, which can accelerate the batter.

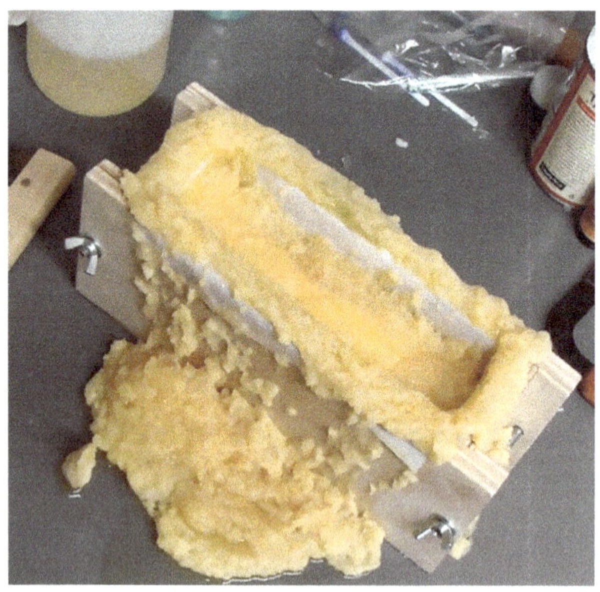

Soap Volcano

The Solution – Simply avoid floral fragrance oils, as they are the most common culprits. Also, work with lye and oils when they are at low temperatures. As you must have surmised by now, high heat + floral fragrance oils = soap issues. Thus, use tried and tested fragrances. If the soap volcanoes out right in front of you, get to work immediately and transfer the soap back into the mold.

Conclusion

Hopefully, after reading this book, you will see that it's not all that tough to make soap. The ingredients may seem dangerous and even confuse you. If you're not sure even now, start with M&P before you meddle with HP and CP soaps. Never forget to purchase all the safety equipment – seriously, this is the most important thing you can do!

If you do follow all the basic rules, you'll end up with soap – soap made with natural oils and without chemicals. Do not be afraid to play with recipes, but test them with small batches so you don't lose too much if something goes wrong. If you decide to take this to the next level, the handmade soap market is waiting for you.

Do not let anything stop you, and you'll soon realize that you're addicted to making soap!

🌟 Join Our Crafting Community! 🌟

Hello Creative Soul,

If you've found joy and inspiration in the pages of our book, we've got something special for you. Become a part of our exclusive mailing list! It's more than just an email subscription; it's your gateway to a world of crafting wonders. Here's what you'll get:

📘 **Exclusive Sneak Peeks**: Be the first to see what's coming. Get early glimpses of our upcoming books that continue to explore the art of crafting.

🎨 **Personalized Content**: Tailored tips, tricks, and tutorials that resonate with your crafting journey. Enhance your skills with content you can't find anywhere else.

📚 **Member-Only Offers**: Enjoy special discounts, offers, and opportunities exclusive to our subscribers.

📝 **Direct Line to the Author**: Share your thoughts, feedback, and what you'd like to see next.

Your input directly influences our future creations!

Joining is easy! Simply:

1. **Visit the Link: https://bit.ly/3PnRASC**

2. **OR, Use the QR Code:**

*We value your privacy and creativity. Your email will be used solely to enhance your crafting journey with us.